BIG IDEAS
MATH®
Blue

A Common Core Curriculum

Assessment Book

- Pre-Course Test with Item Analysis

- Quizzes

- Chapter Tests

- Standards Assessment with Item Analysis

- Alternative Assessments

- End-of-Course Tests

Erie, Pennsylvania

ISBN 13: 978-1-60840-472-8
ISBN 10: 1-60840-472-2

123456789-VLP-17 16 15 14 13

Contents

About the Assessment Book iv

Pre-Course Test with Item Analysis 1

Chapter 1 Equations 5

Chapter 2 Transformations 17

Chapter 3 Angles and Triangles... 29

Chapter 4 Graphing and Writing Linear Equations.................................... 41

Chapter 5 Systems of Linear Equations... 53

Chapter 6 Functions 65

Chapter 7 Real Numbers and the Pythagorean Theorem 77

Chapter 8 Volume and Similar Solids 89

Chapter 9 Data Analysis and Displays 101

Chapter 10 Exponents and Scientific Notation.. 113

End-of-Course Tests... 125

Gridded Response Answer Sheet... 133

Answers... A1

About the Assessment Book

Pre-Course Test with Item Analysis

The Pre-Course Test covers material that students should be familiar with from earlier courses. The Item Analysis can be used to determine topics that need to be reviewed.

Quizzes

The Quizzes provide ongoing assessment of student understanding. There are two quizzes for each chapter.

Chapter Tests

The Chapter Tests provide assessment of student understanding of key concepts taught in the chapter. There are two tests for each chapter.

Standards Assessment with Item Analysis

The Standards Assessment provides students practice answering questions in state assessment format. The assessments are cumulative and cover material from the current chapter as well as earlier chapters of the textbook. Questions are presented in multiple choice, gridded response, short response, and extended response format. The Item Analysis can be used to identify common errors and assess student understanding.

Alternative Assessment with Scoring Rubric

Each Alternative Assessment includes at least one multi-step problem that combines a variety of concepts from the chapter. Students are asked to explain their solutions, write about the mathematics, or compare and analyze different situations.

End-of-Course Tests

The End-of-Course Tests cover the key concepts taught throughout the course and can be used as a year-end exam or as a practice test to help students prepare for state assessments.

Gridded Response Answer Sheet

The Gridded Response Answer Sheets can be used to help students practice completing gridded response questions.

Name_____ Date_____

Tell whether the two fractions form a proportion.

Answers

1. $\dfrac{3}{4}, \dfrac{16}{20}$ **2.** $\dfrac{5}{7}, \dfrac{30}{42}$ **3.** $\dfrac{4}{18}, \dfrac{6}{27}$

4. Use the ratio table to find the unit rate in dollars per ounce.

Amount (ounces)	12	16	20	24
Cost (dollars)	0.96	1.28	1.6	1.92

Order the numbers from least to greatest.

5. $\left|-5\right|, 6, -6, -\left|4\right|, -2$ **6.** $\dfrac{15}{2}, -8.5, -\dfrac{42}{5}, 10.2$

Solve the inequality.

7. $4x < 24$ **8.** $x + 8 \geq 12$

9. What is the volume of the prism?

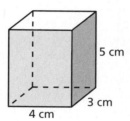

5 cm
3 cm
4 cm

10. A map has a scale of 1 in. : 10 mi. On the map, the distance between two cities is 5 inches. What is the actual distance between the cities?

Simplify the expression.

11. $-4 + 11$ **12.** $-6 - 9$ **13.** $-7(-8)$

14. $60 \div (-4)$ **15.** $\left|-34\right|$ **16.** $\left|-(-41)\right|$

17. $17(-14)$ **18.** $12 - (-19)$ **19.** $\dfrac{4}{15} + \dfrac{5}{9}$

20. $-\dfrac{7}{8} \div \dfrac{3}{4}$ **21.** $\dfrac{13}{18} \bullet \dfrac{9}{25}$ **22.** $-\dfrac{7}{12} - \dfrac{1}{8}$

23. $(0.6)^2$ **24.** $8.37(-5.3)$ **25.** $0.95 - 3.49$

1. _____
2. _____
3. _____
4. _____
5. _____
6. _____
7. _____
8. _____
9. _____
10. _____
11. _____
12. _____
13. _____
14. _____
15. _____
16. _____
17. _____
18. _____
19. _____
20. _____
21. _____
22. _____
23. _____
24. _____
25. _____

Name _____ Date _____

26. The length and the width of a rectangle are both doubled. What is the ratio of the area of the larger rectangle to the area of the smaller rectangle?

Solve the equation.

27. $7 + x = -2$ **28.** $8 - x = 13$ **29.** $x - 11 = -5$

30. $3x - 2 = -5$ **31.** $8x + 5 = 21$ **32.** $9 - 2x = 23$

33. Use the properties of equality to show that the equation $6x + 3 = 27$ is equivalent to the equation $2x = 8$.

Find the coordinates of the point.

34. A **35.** B

36. C **37.** D

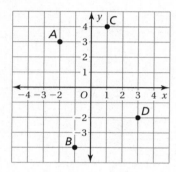

Complete the statement using <, >, or =.

38. 1 in. ____ 2.54 cm   **39.** 40 in. ____ 1 m   **40.** 7 L ____ 2 gal

Write the fraction as a decimal.

41. $\dfrac{3}{4}$ **42.** $\dfrac{5}{16}$ **43.** $\dfrac{21}{4}$

44. In a class, the teacher asks each person wearing red to name his or her favorite color. Is this sample representative of the entire class? Explain.

45. The data below are the test scores of the students in a math class.

   97, 76, 84, 82, 90, 95, 77, 79, 80, 82, 84, 77, 100, 78, 87

Create a stem-and-leaf plot to represent the data.

46. Each of the letters in the word MATHEMATICS are written on separate index cards. The cards are then placed in a hat. What is the probability of randomly drawing an index card with a vowel on it from the hat?

Answers

26. _____

27. _____

28. _____

29. _____

30. _____

31. _____

32. _____

33. _____

34. _____

35. _____

36. _____

37. _____

38. ____See left.____

39. ____See left.____

40. ____See left.____

41. _____

42. _____

43. _____

44. _____

_____

_____

45. ____See left.____

46. _____

Item Number	Skills
1	simplifying fractions, understanding proportion
2	simplifying fractions, understanding proportion
3	simplifying fractions, understanding proportion
4	using a ratio table to find a unit rate
5	ordering rational numbers
6	ordering rational numbers
7	solving one-step inequalities
8	solving one-step inequalities
9	finding the volume of a prism
10	understanding scale
11	adding integers
12	subtracting integers
13	multiplying integers
14	dividing integers
15	finding absolute value of integers
16	finding absolute value of integers
17	multiplying integers
18	subtracting integers
19	adding fractions
20	dividing fractions
21	multiplying fractions
22	subtracting fractions
23	raising a decimal to a power

Item Number	Skills
24	multiplying decimals
25	subtracting decimals
26	understanding how changes in linear dimensions affect the area of a figure
27	solving one-step equations
28	solving one-step equations
29	solving one-step equations
30	solving two-step equations
31	solving two-step equations
32	solving two-step equations
33	using properties of equality
34	identifying the coordinates of a point
35	identifying the coordinates of a point
36	identifying the coordinates of a point
37	identifying the coordinates of a point
38	converting between metric and customary
39	converting between metric and customary
40	converting between metric and customary
41	writing a fraction as a decimal
42	writing a fraction as a decimal
43	writing a fraction as a decimal
44	evaluating a sample
45	making a stem-and-leaf plot
46	theoretical probability

Name_____ Date _____

Solve the equation. Check your solution.

Answers

1. $4 - c = -\dfrac{1}{3}$

2. $-14 = x - 12$

1. _____

2. _____

3. $\dfrac{s}{1.5} = 0.8$

4. $0.4r = 1.6$

3. _____

4. _____

Solve the equation. Check your solution.

5. $2d - 15 = 3$

6. $4 = \dfrac{3}{4}m - 6$

5. _____

6. _____

7. $-3(n + 6) + 10 = -8$

8. $1.5(q - 4) - 2 = 4$

7. _____

8. _____

Find the value of x. Then find the angle measures of the polygon.

9. _____

9.
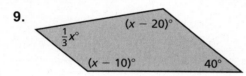
Sum of angle measures: 360°

10.
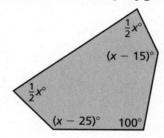
Sum of angle measures: 540°

10. _____

11. The equation $R = 10A - 20$ represents the revenue R (in dollars) you make by spending A dollars on advertising. Your revenue totaled $110. How much did you spend on advertising?

11. _____

12. _____

12. A 150-foot fence encloses a garden. What is the length of each side of the garden?

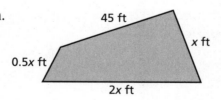

13. _____

13. A car drives 60 miles per hour. Write and solve an equation to find the number of hours it takes the car to travel 360 miles.

14. _____

14. Use the table to write and solve an equation to find the number of cars c that a salesperson needs to sell in the fourth month so that the salesperson's mean number of cars sold per month is 10.

Month	1	2	3	4
Cars Sold	8	9	12	c

Chapter 1 Quiz
For use after Section 1.4

Solve the equation. Check your solution, if possible.

Answers

1. $-4p = 3p + 28$

2. $-2y - 4 = 4(y - 1)$

3. $3(k + 5) = -2(3k - 6)$

4. $\frac{1}{2}r + 4 = \frac{3}{4}r - \frac{3}{2}$

5. $2a - 9 = 2a + 5$

6. $8m + 2 + 4m = 2(6m + 1)$

Solve the equation for _y_.

7. $5x - 4y = 10$

8. $7 = -y + 3x$

9. The formula for the volume V of a cone is $V = \frac{1}{3}\pi r^2 h$. Solve the formula for the height h.

10. The formula for the area A of a triangle is $A = \frac{1}{2}bh$. Solve the formula for the base length b.

11. It is 35°C at your school and 90°F at home. Where is the temperature higher?

12. The area of a trapezoid is $A = \frac{1}{2}h(b + B)$. Solve the formula for the height h. What is the height if the area is 200 square feet, the length of the smaller base b is 10 feet, and the length of the larger base B is 15 feet?

13. From your home, the route to the school that passes the mall is 2 miles shorter than the route to the school that passes the theater. What is the length of each route?

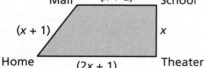

Mall ___(x + 2)___ School
(x + 1)   x
Home ___(2x + 1)___ Theater

14. The formula for the surface area S of a cylinder is $S = 2\pi r^2 + 2\pi rh$. Solve the formula for the height h.

1. _____

2. _____

3. _____

4. _____

5. _____

6. _____

7. _____

8. _____

9. _____

10. _____

11. _____

12. _____

_____

13. _____

_____

14. _____

Name_____ Date _____

Chapter 1 Test A

Solve the equation. Check your solution, if possible.

1. $y - 12 = 9$

2. $42 = 7x$

3. $5p - 7 = 28$

4. $1.5x + 1.3x = -8.4$

5. $\dfrac{4}{3}w - 12 = \dfrac{2}{3}w$

6. $4(3q - 2) = 16q$

7. $-h + 4 = -h + 9$

8. $t + 3t - 7 = 4t - 7$

9. $\dfrac{1}{4}(n - 6) = \dfrac{1}{4}n - \dfrac{3}{2}$

10. $2d + \dfrac{1}{6} = 6\left(\dfrac{1}{3}d + 1\right)$

Solve the equation for y.

11. $\dfrac{2}{5}x + y = 3$

12. $8 = 3x + 6y$

13. $1.5x - 3y = 6$

14. $\dfrac{1}{4}y - 2x = 5$

15. The formula for profit is $P = R - C$.

    a. Solve the formula for R.

    b. Use the new formula to find the value of R given that $P = \$350$ and $C = \$520$.

Solve the formula for the bold variable.

16. $V = \ell w\mathbf{h}$

17. $s = \mathbf{p} - 0.2t$

18. $Z = s\mathbf{L}$

19. $PV = nR\mathbf{T}$

Find the value of x. Then find the angle measures of the polygon.

20.

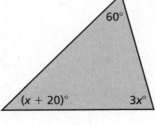

Sum of angle
measures: 180°

21.

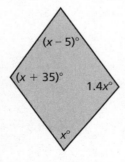

Sum of angle
measures: 360°

Answers

1. _____

2. _____

3. _____

4. _____

5. _____

6. _____

7. _____

8. _____

9. _____

10. _____

11. _____

12. _____

13. _____

14. _____

15. a._____

    b._____

16. _____

17. _____

18. _____

19. _____

20. _____

_____

_____

_____

21. _____

_____

_____

Chapter 1 Test A (continued)

22. There are 24 more students in the seventh grade class than the number g in the eighth grade class. The seventh grade class has 160 students. Write and solve an equation to find the number of students in the eighth grade class.

23. You rent a canoe for $5 per hour. Your cost before the tax is added is $12.50. Write and solve an equation to find the number of hours that you rented the canoe.

24. The cost (in dollars) of making n birthday cakes is represented by $C = 24n + 35$. How many birthday cakes are made when the cost is $395? Explain your reasoning.

Answers

22. _____

_____

23. _____

_____

24. _____See left._____

25. _____

26. _____

_____

_____

27. a._____

b._____

25. Find the perimeter of the square.

4x + 3 in.

3(2x − 5) in.

26. George makes a $1000 down payment for a car and then pays $325 per month. Elaine makes a $2500 down payment for a car and then pays $325 per month. Is there any number of months after which both George and Elaine will have paid the same amount? Explain.

27. The area of the trapezoidal car window is given by $A = \frac{1}{2}h(b + B)$.

a. Solve the formula for B.

b. Use the new formula to find B when b is 22 inches, h is 20 inches, and the area is 500 square inches.

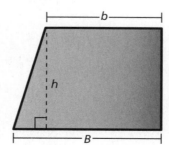

Name _____ Date _____

Solve the equation. Check your solution, if possible.

Answers

1. $-26d = -364$

2. $x - \dfrac{1}{3} = \dfrac{2}{5}$

3. $4\pi = s + 5\pi$

4. $\dfrac{3}{5}w - \dfrac{1}{5}w + 10 = 4$

5. $4(3 - 6a) = 36$

6. $4(2g - 3) = 5(g - 2)$

7. $6r - 8 = 8 + 6r$

8. $\dfrac{2}{3}y + 6 = \dfrac{2}{3}(y + 9)$

9. $0.4(15p + 6) = 1.5(4p + 1.6)$ **10.** $9n - 4 + n = 5 + 10n$

Solve the equation for y.

11. $2\pi = 5x - 3y$

12. $2.4x - 1.5y = 3$

13. $2.7 = 5.4y - 8.1x$

14. $\dfrac{1}{3}x + \dfrac{2}{3}y = 1$

15. The formula for simple interest is $I = Prt$.

 a. Solve the formula for P.

 b. Use the new formula to find the value of P in the table.

I	$40
P	?
r	4%
t	2

Solve the formula for the bold variable.

16. $i = \dfrac{e\mathbf{c}}{3}$

17. $P = 2\ell + 2\mathbf{w}$

18. $I = \dfrac{V}{\mathbf{R}}$

19. $S = 3\pi r^2 + 2\pi r\mathbf{h}$

Find the value of x. Then find the angle measures of the polygon.

20.

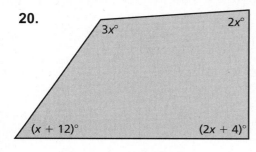

Sum of angle measures: 360°

21.

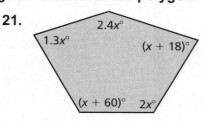

Sum of angle measures: 540°

1. _____
2. _____
3. _____
4. _____
5. _____
6. _____
7. _____
8. _____
9. _____
10. _____
11. _____
12. _____
13. _____
14. _____
15. a._____

 b._____

16. _____
17. _____
18. _____
19. _____
20. _____

 _____

 _____

 _____

21. _____

 _____

 _____

Chapter 1 **Test B** (continued)

22. The cost of your new book bag is $11.50 more than the cost c of your old book bag. You pay $47 for your new book bag. Write and solve an equation to find the cost of your old book bag.

23. You can rent a video game for $3.50. Your total cost of rentals for the month was $31.50. Write and solve an equation to find the number of video game rentals for the month.

24. You purchase 5 movies and a CD. The cost of the CD is $8.50. Your total bill before tax is $38.45. Write and solve an equation to find the cost of a movie.

25. The formula $C = p + 0.06p$ represents the after-tax cost C for an item with a purchase price p.

    a. Solve for p.

    b. Find the purchase price if the after-tax cost is $62.54.

26. Are there any values of x for which the areas of the two rectangles are the same? Explain. Are there any values of x for which the perimeters of the two rectangles are the same? If so, find such a value of x.

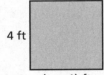
4 ft
(x + 1) ft

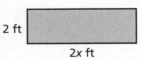
2 ft
2x ft

Answers

22. _____

    _____

23. _____

    _____

24. _____

    _____

25. a. _____

    b. _____

26. _____

    _____

    _____

    _____

    _____

27. a. _____

    b. _____

27. The volume of a right circular cone is given by $V = \dfrac{\pi r^2 h}{3}$.

    a. Solve the formula for h.

    b. Which is greater, the height or the radius of the cone?

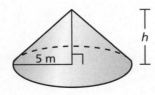
5 m
h
$V = 150\ m^3$

Chapter 1   **Standards Assessment**

1. What value of x makes the equation below true?

    $$5x + 9 = x + 20$$

    A. 7.25   **C.** 2.75

    B. 5.8   **D.** 2.2

2. **GRIDDED RESPONSE** The square shown below has a perimeter of $6x - 20$ units. What is the value of x?

3. The formula $PV = 300R$ is used in chemistry. How can this formula be solved for P?

    F. Divide both sides of the formula by P.

    G. Divide both sides of the formula by V.

    H. Subtract P from both sides of the formula.

    I. Subtract V from both sides of the formula.

4. Emma received a $40 gift card that could be used to download television programs. After she downloaded 5 programs, she had $30 remaining on her gift card. If each program costs the same amount to download, what is the cost of one download?

    A. $2   **C.** $8

    B. $6   **D.** $10

5. Which of the following equations is equivalent to the equation $30 = -2(-2x + 6)$?

    F. $30 = 4x + 12$ **H.** $30 = 4x + 6$

    G. $30 = 4x - 12$ **I.** $30 = 4x - 6$

Chapter 1 **Standards Assessment** (continued)

6. The drawing shows equal weights on two sides of a balance scale.

The can of coffee weighs 20 ounces. Each book weighs 36 ounces. What is the weight, in ounces, of one carton of salt?

A. 8 **C.** 46

B. 26 **D.** 52

7. Which of the following describes a correct method for solving the equation below?

$$-\frac{1}{2} = 6 - \frac{2}{3}x$$

F. Add 6 to both sides, then divide both sides by $\frac{3}{2}$.

G. Subtract 6 from both sides, then multiply both sides by $-\frac{2}{3}$.

H. Add −6 to both sides, then multiply both sides by $-\frac{3}{2}$.

I. Subtract 6 from both sides, then add $\frac{2}{3}$ to both sides.

8. **EXTENDED RESPONSE** You need $329.99 for a new digital camera. You have $25.75 and will save $23.50 each week.

Part A Write an equation to represent the number of weeks it will take for you to save enough money for a new digital camera.

Part B After how many weeks will you have enough money for a new digital camera? Explain your reasoning.

1. **A.** The student adds 9 and 20 instead of subtracting.

   B. The student adds 9 and 20 instead of subtracting, and then miscalculates $5x - x$, ignoring the coefficient of x.

   C. Correct answer

   D. The student calculates $20 - 9$ correctly, but then miscalculates $5x - x$, ignoring the coefficient of x.

2. Correct answer: 10

   Common error: The student confuses or does not know the meaning of perimeter and sets x equal to $6x - 20$, yielding the answer $x = 4$.

3. **F.** The student misunderstands what it means to solve for P.

   G. Correct answer

   H. The student misunderstands what it means to solve for P and thinks that PV can be separated using subtraction.

   I. The student thinks that PV can be separated using subtraction instead of division.

4. **A.** Correct answer

   B. The student divides $30 by 5.

   C. The student divides $40 by 5.

   D. The student subtracts the two dollar amounts given in the problem, $40 - $30.

5. **F.** The student incorrectly distributes the negative sign to the second term inside the parentheses, getting 12 instead of −12.

   G. Correct answer

   H. The student does not distribute the −2 to the second term inside the parentheses, leaving it as 6.

   I. The student distributes only the negative sign but not the 2 to the second term inside the parentheses, getting −6.

6. **A.** The student only accounts for one book on the right side.

   B. Correct answer

   C. The student adds the weight of the coffee can to that of the books instead of subtracting it.

   D. The student correctly subtracts the coffee can from the two books but fails to divide the result by 2.

7. **F.** The student adds 6 to both sides instead of subtracting, and then divides both sides by $\dfrac{3}{2}$ instead of $-\dfrac{2}{3}$.

   G. The student multiplies both sides by $-\dfrac{2}{3}$ instead of dividing.

   H. Correct answer

   I. The student thinks that $-\dfrac{2}{3}x$ means subtraction and that the required inverse operation is addition.

8. **4 points** The student demonstrates a thorough understanding of writing and solving two-step equations. For Part A, the student correctly writes the equation $329.99 = 25.75 + 23.50x$ and provides an appropriate explanation. For Part B, the student correctly gets a value of approximately 13, shows appropriate work, and states that they will need to save money for 13 weeks.

   3 points The student demonstrates an understanding of writing and solving two-step equations, but the student's work and explanations demonstrate an essential but less than thorough understanding.

   2 points The student demonstrates a partial understanding of writing and solving two-step equations. The student's work and explanations demonstrate a lack of essential understanding.

   1 point The student demonstrates a limited understanding of writing and solving two-step equations. The student's response is incomplete and exhibits many flaws.

   0 points The student provides no response, a complete incorrect or incomprehensible response, or a response that demonstrates insufficient understanding of writing and solving two-step equations.

Name_____ Date_____

 Alternative Assessment

1. Linda likes to figure out how number puzzles work. Just this week, she learned about two new puzzles and is trying to work them out. See if you can help her.

   a. Puzzle 1

   I am thinking of a number. Multiplying it by 7 and adding 2 is equal to multiplying it by 2 and adding 7. What is the number?

   Use an equation to find the answer. Then explain or show why you can substitute any number you choose both for 7 and for 2.

   b. Puzzle 2

   Choose a number. Multiply it by 4. Add 8 to the product. Divide the sum by 4. Tell me what number you have now.

   What must be done to figure out what number you chose? Use algebra to show how to find the original number choice.

Name _____ Date _____

Score	Conceptual Understanding	Mathematical Skills	Work Habits
4	Shows complete understanding of: • writing equations • solving equations	Writes and solves the equations correctly and accurately for the two puzzle situations.	Answers all parts of all problems. All equations are written in a systematic way. Work is very neat and well organized.
3	Shows nearly complete understanding of: • writing equations • solving equations	Writes and solves the equations correctly and accurately for the two puzzle situations.	Answers almost all parts of all questions. Most equations are written in a systematic way. Work is neat and organized.
2	Shows some understanding of: • writing equations • solving equations	Writes and solves an equation correctly and accurately for one puzzle situation.	Answers some parts of all questions. Some equations are written in a systematic way. Work is not very neat or organized.
1	Shows little understanding of: • writing equations • solving equations	Does not write or solve the equation correctly for any puzzle.	Does not attempt any part of any problem. No equations are written. Work is sloppy and disorganized.

Name _____ Date _____

Chapter 2 **Quiz**
For use after Section 2.4

Tell whether the two figures are congruent. Explain your reasoning.

Answers

1.

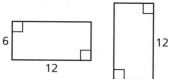

2.

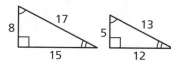

Tell whether the shaded figure is a translation of the nonshaded figure.

3.

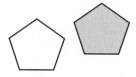

4.

Tell whether the shaded figure is a reflection of the nonshaded figure.

5.

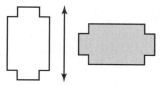

6.

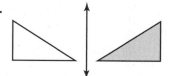

The shaded figure is congruent to the nonshaded figure. Describe two different sequences of transformations in which the nonshaded figure is the image of the shaded figure.

7.

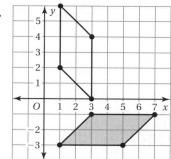

8.

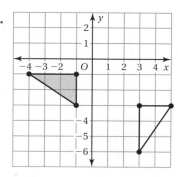

1. _____

   _____

2. _____

   _____

3. _____

4. _____

5. _____

6. _____

7. _____

   _____

   _____

   _____

8. _____

   _____

   _____

9. _____

10. _____

9. The vertices of a triangle are $A(-2, 4)$, $B(1, 2)$, and $C(-2, -2)$. Reflect the triangle in the y-axis, and then rotate the image 90° counterclockwise about the origin. What are the coordinates of the image?

10. The vertices of a rectangle are $W(2, 2)$, $X(4, 3)$, $Y(5, 2)$, and $Z(4, 1)$. Reflect the figure in the y-axis, and then translate the image 3 units right and 4 units down. What are the coordinates of the image?

Copyright © Big Ideas Learning, LLC
All rights reserved.

Big Ideas Math Blue **17**
Assessment Book

Chapter 2 **Quiz**
For use after Section 2.7

1. Tell whether the two triangles are similar. Explain your reasoning.

 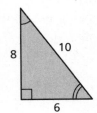

Answers

1. _____

_____

2. _____

3. _____

The polygons are similar. Find x.

2.

3.

4. _____

_____

5. _____

_____

The two figures are similar. Find the ratios (shaded to nonshaded) of the perimeters and of the areas.

6. _____

7. _____

4.

5.

8. _____

9. _____

_____

_____

Tell whether the shaded figure is a dilation of the nonshaded figure.

6.

7.

8. The front of the speaker is similar to the front of a speaker in a photo. What is the area of the front of the speaker?

3 in.
Area = 6 in.²
18 in.

9. The vertices of a triangle are $A(-4, 2)$, $B(-4, -4)$, and $C(6, -4)$.

Dilate the triangle with respect to the origin using a scale factor of $\frac{1}{2}$.

Then reflect in the x-axis. What are the coordinates of the image?

Name_____ Date _____

Triangles *ABC* and *QRS* are congruent.

Answers

1. Which angle of *ABC* corresponds to $\angle R$?

2. Which angle of *QRS* corresponds to $\angle A$?

3. Which side of *ABC* corresponds to side *SQ*?

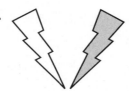

1. _____

2. _____

3. _____

4. _____

Tell whether the shaded figure is a *translation, reflection, rotation,* or *dilation* of the nonshaded figure.

5. _____

4.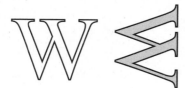

5.

6. _____

7. _____

6.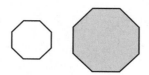

8. _____

7.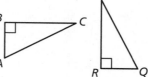

_____

_____

_____

9. _____

8. The vertices of a rectangle are $A(2, 0)$, $B(5, 0)$, $C(5, -2)$, and $D(2, -2)$. Reflect the rectangle in the *y*-axis, and then rotate the rectangle 180° about the origin. What are the coordinates of the image?

_____

_____

_____

10. __**See left.**__

9. The vertices of a triangle are $X(-3, 3)$, $Y(-1, 3)$, and $Z(-3, 0)$. Dilate the triangle with respect to the origin using a scale factor of 2. Then translate the image 5 units right and 1 unit down. What are the coordinates of the image?

_____

_____

_____

10. Rotate the triangle 180° about the origin. Find the coordinates of the image.

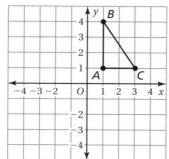

Chapter 2 **Test A** (continued)

Tell whether the two figures are similar. Explain your reasoning.

11.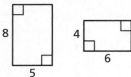

12.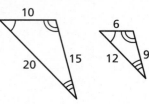

Answers

11. _____

   _____

12. _____

   _____

The two figures are similar. Find the ratios (small to large) of the perimeters and of the areas.

13.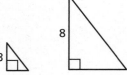

14.

13. _____

14. _____

15. _____

16. a. _____

   b. _____

   c. _____

17. _____

18. _____

15. Figure A is a dilation of Figure B by a scale factor of 3. What is the scale factor of Figure B to Figure A?

16. A map of your neighborhood is represented on the grid.

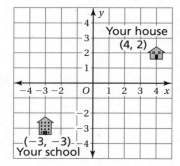

   a. Describe a translation of your walk from school to your house.

   b. The pizza parlor is a reflection in the y-axis of your school. What are the coordinates of the pizza parlor?

   c. The transformation from your house to the park is a 90° clockwise rotation about the origin. What are the coordinates of the park?

17. The scale on a map is 1 in. : 50 mi. The actual distance between two cities is 350 miles. What is the distance between the cities on the map?

18. The ratio of the corresponding side lengths of two similar MP3 players is 4 : 3. The area of the larger MP3 player is 8 square inches. What is the area of the smaller MP3 player?

Name_____ Date_____

Trapezoids *ABCD* and *EFGH* are congruent.

Answers

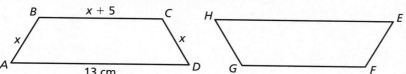

1. Which side of *EFGH* is congruent to side *AD*?

2. The perimeter of *ABCD* is 30 centimeters. What is the value of *x*?

3. What is the length of side *EF*?

4. What is the length of side *GF*?

Tell whether the shaded figure is a *translation, reflection, rotation,* or *dilation* of the nonshaded figure.

5.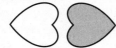

6.

7.

8.

1. _____
2. _____
3. _____
4. _____
5. _____
6. _____
7. _____
8. _____
9. _____

_____

_____

10. ___**See left.**___

_____

_____

_____

9. The vertices of a triangle are $X(-6, -9)$, $Y(-3, -9)$, and $Z(-3, -3)$.

   Dilate the triangle with respect to the origin using a scale factor of $\frac{1}{3}$.

   Then reflect the triangle in the *x*-axis. What are the coordinates of the image?

10. Rotate the triangle 180° about the origin, and then translate the triangle 3 units right and 2 units up. Find the coordinates of the image.

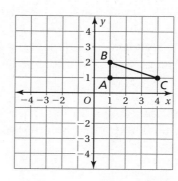

Chapter 2 **Test B** (continued)

The polygons are similar. Find x.

11.

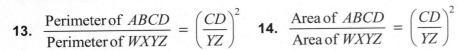

12.

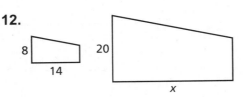

Answers

11. _____

_____

12. _____

_____

Rectangle ABCD is similar to Rectangle WXYZ. Tell whether the statement is *true* or *false*.

13. $\dfrac{\text{Perimeter of } ABCD}{\text{Perimeter of } WXYZ} = \left(\dfrac{CD}{YZ}\right)^2$ 14. $\dfrac{\text{Area of } ABCD}{\text{Area of } WXYZ} = \left(\dfrac{CD}{YZ}\right)^2$

13. _____

14. _____

15. a. _____

15. Several transformations are used to create the quilt.

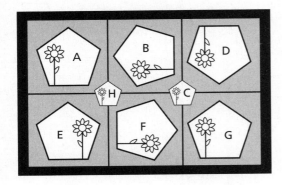

b. _____

c. _____

d. _____

e. _____

16. _____

_____

17. _____

18. _____

    a. Describe the transformation of Design A to Design B.

    b. Describe the transformation of Design E to Design G.

    c. Describe the transformation of Design A to Design H.

    d. Which two designs represent a translation?

    e. From Design A, which design is a reflection and a 90° clockwise rotation about the origin?

16. Explain how you know if a dilation is an enlargement or a reduction.

17. The ratio of the side length of Square A to the side length of Square B is 3 : 5. The perimeter of Square B is 60 feet. What is the area of Square A?

18. A scale on a drawing is 0.5 mm : 4 cm. The height of the drawing is 4.5 millimeters. What is the actual height of the object?

Name_____ Date_____

1. The figures are similar.

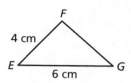 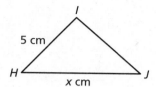

What is the value of x?

A. 4.8

C. 7.5

B. 7

D. 8

2. GRIDDED RESPONSE Rectangle $ABCD$ is graphed on the coordinate grid below.

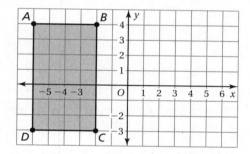

Reflect Rectangle $ABCD$ over the y-axis. What is the x-coordinate of point A'?

3. Ben was solving the equation in the box shown. What should Ben do to correct the error that he made?

F. Add $\dfrac{3}{4}$ to each side to get $-5x = \dfrac{5}{12}$.

G. Subtract $\dfrac{3}{4}$ from each side to get $-5x = -\dfrac{4}{7}$.

H. Divide each side by -5 to get $x + \dfrac{3}{4} = \dfrac{1}{15}$.

I. Multiply each side by $-\dfrac{1}{5}$ to get $x = \dfrac{13}{60}$.

$$-5x + \frac{3}{4} = -\frac{1}{3}$$

$$-5x + \frac{3}{4} - \frac{3}{4} = -\frac{1}{3} - \frac{3}{4}$$

$$-5x = -\frac{13}{12}$$

$$\frac{1}{5} \cdot (-5x) = \left(-\frac{13}{12}\right) \cdot \frac{1}{5}$$

$$x = -\frac{13}{60}$$

Chapter 2 **Standards Assessment** (continued)

4. The vertices of a triangle are $A(8, -24)$, $B(8, -8)$, and $C(16, -8)$. If the triangle is dilated by a scale factor of $\frac{1}{4}$, what will be the coordinates of A'?

   A. $(32, -56)$ **C.** $(2, -2)$

   B. $(4, -2)$ **D.** $(2, -6)$

5. Which description is the correct way to solve the equation below?

   $$7x - 3 = -31$$

   F. Add 3 to both sides then divide both sides by 7.

   G. Subtract 3 from both sides then divide both sides by 7.

   H. Add 3 to both sides then multiply both sides by 7.

   I. Subtract 3 from both sides then multiply both sides by 7.

6. Mr. Glidden is expanding the size of his garden. His new garden will be 3 times as long and 2 times as wide as his original garden.

   The perimeter of his original garden is 30 feet and the length is 11 feet. What will be the perimeter, in feet, of his new garden?

   A. 75   **C.** 142

   B. 82   **D.** 180

7. **SHORT RESPONSE** Rectangle *ABCD* is similar to Rectangle *JKLM*.

   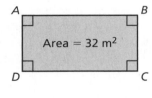
   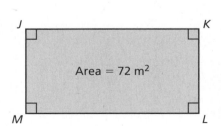

   Part A   What is the ratio (*ABCD* to *JKLM*) of the corresponding side lengths?

   Part B   Side *BC* is 4 meters long. Side *CD* is twice the length of side *BC*. What is the length of side *LM*? Explain your reasoning.

1. **A.** The student reverses the given ratio and divides 6 by 1.25 instead of multiplying.

    B. Because $\overline{HI}$ is 1 centimeter longer than $\overline{EF}$, the student thinks that $\overline{HJ}$ is 1 centimeter longer than $\overline{EG}$.

    C. Correct answer

    D. The student chooses an answer based only on visual approximation.

2. Correct answer: 6

    Common error: The student reflects the rectangle across the x-axis and answers -6.

3. **F.** The student forgets that subtraction is the inverse operation of addition.

    G. The student subtracts the numerators and the denominators instead of finding a common denominator.

    H. The student forgets to divide $\frac{3}{4}$ by -5.

    I. Correct answer

4. **A.** The student multiplies the coordinates of point A by 4 instead of dividing by 4.

    B. The student finds the coordinates of point C'.

    C. The student finds the coordinates of point B'.

    D. Correct answer

5. **F.** Correct answer

    G. The student forgets that the inverse operation of subtraction is addition.

    H. The student forgets that the inverse operation of multiplication is division.

    I. The student forgets that the inverse operation of subtraction is addition and that the inverse operation of multiplication is division.

6. **A.** The student averages the two scale factors given and multiplies the original perimeter by 2.5.

    B. Correct answer

    C. The student subtracts the original length from the original perimeter, instead of from half the original perimeter, to get an original width of 19. The student then finds the new length of 33 and an incorrect new width of 38. The student then uses these measurements to get a perimeter of 142.

    D. The student uses the scale factors incorrectly and multiplies the original perimeter by 3 and then that product by 2.

7. **2 points** The student demonstrates a thorough understanding of similar figures. First, the student uses the given information to find the ratio of the corresponding side lengths, $\frac{2}{3}$. Next, the student finds that the length of side *LM* is 12 meters.

The student explains that side *CD* has a length of 8 meters from the given information and then uses the ratio of corresponding side lengths to find the length of side *LM*.

1 point The student demonstrates a partial understanding of similar figures. For example, the student correctly finds the ratio of the corresponding side lengths, but uses the wrong side when finding the length of side *LM*.

0 points The student demonstrates insufficient understanding of similar figures. The student might forget to find the square root of the ratio of the areas or be unable to use the given information to solve the problem.

Chapter 2 **Alternative Assessment**

1. **a.** The vertices of a quadrilateral are $P(-6, 6)$, $Q(-2, 6)$, $R(-2, 2)$, and $S(-6, 2)$. Graph Quadrilateral $PQRS$.

   b. Reflect $PQRS$ in the y-axis. What are the coordinates of the image?

   c. Reflect the image from part (b) in the x-axis. What are the coordinates of the image?

   d. Reflect the image from part (c) in the y-axis. What are the coordinates of the image?

   e. Describe how the image from part (d) could result from one transformation of $PQRS$.

   f. You formed three images by using three reflections. Describe other transformations or combinations of transformations to $PQRS$ that would produce the same three images without using reflections.

2. **a.** The vertices of a triangle are $L(-3, 3)$, $M(6, 0)$, and $N(-3, -6)$. Graph Triangle LMN.

   b. Triangle ABC is a dilation of Triangle LMN. The vertices of Triangle ABC are $A(-1, 1)$, $B(2, 0)$, and $C(-1, -2)$. Graph Triangle ABC. Identify the type of dilation and find the scale factor.

   c. The image of Triangle LMN after dilation with a scale factor of 2 is Triangle XYZ. Graph Triangle XYZ and identify the type of dilation.

   d. You graphed the vertices of three triangles. Describe the dilation from Triangle ABC to Triangle XYZ and find the scale factor. Describe the dilation from Triangle XYZ to Triangle ABC and find the scale factor. What do you notice about the scale factors?

Chapter 2 Alternative Assessment Rubric

Score	Conceptual Understanding	Mathematical Skills	Work Habits
4	Shows complete understanding of: • translations, reflections, and rotations in the coordinate plane • dilations in the coordinate plane	Reflects three images correctly and identifies other transformations. Dilates two images and correctly identifies the scale factors.	Answers all parts of each problem. Graphing in the coordinate plane is done carefully and points are accurately identified. Work is very neat and well organized.
3	Shows nearly complete understanding of: • translations, reflections, and rotations in the coordinate plane • dilations in the coordinate plane	Reflects two images correctly and identifies another transformation. Dilates two images correctly and identifies one scale factor.	Answers most parts of each problem. Most graphing in the coordinate plane is done carefully and most points are accurately identified. Work is neat and organized.
2	Shows some understanding of: • translations, reflections, and rotations in the coordinate plane • dilations in the coordinate plane	Identifies two similar quadrilaterals but does not generate another one. Dilates one image correctly and identifies one scale factor.	Answers some parts of each problem. Some graphing in the coordinate plane is done carefully and some points are accurately identified. Work is sloppy and not well organized.
1	Shows little understanding of: • translations, reflections, and rotations in the coordinate plane • dilations in the coordinate plane	Does not identify similar quadrilaterals or generate another quadrilateral. Does not dilate images or identify the scale factors.	Answers few parts of each problem. Graphing in the coordinate plane is not done carefully and points are inaccurately identified. Work is sloppy and disorganized.

Chapter 3 **Quiz**
For use after Section 3.2

Use the figure to find the measure of the angle. Explain your reasoning.

1. ∠3   2. ∠5

3. ∠6   4. ∠2

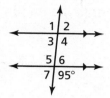

Answers

1. _____

   _____

2. _____

   _____

Complete the statement. Explain your reasoning.

5. If the measure of ∠3 = 46°,
   then the measure of ∠6 = __?__.

6. If the measure of ∠5 = 102°,
   then the measure of ∠8 = __?__.

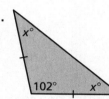

3. _____

   _____

7. If the measure of ∠4 = 98°, then the measure of ∠7 = __?__.

8. If the measure of ∠6 = 59°, then the measure of ∠4 = __?__.

4. _____

   _____

5. _____

Find the measures of the interior angles.

9.   10.   11.

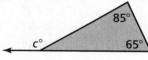
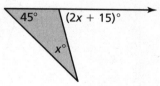

   _____

6. _____

   _____

7. _____

Find the measure of the exterior angle.

12.   13.

   _____

8. _____

14. A lectern has four vertical sides and
    a slanted top. Find the measures
    of ∠1 and ∠2. Explain your reasoning.

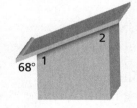

   _____

9. _____

10. _____

11. _____

12. _____

13. _____

14. _____

15. A ladder leaning against a wall forms
    a triangle and exterior angles with
    the wall and the ground. What are the
    measures of the exterior angles?
    Justify your answer.

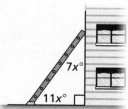

15. _____

   _____

Name _____ Date _____

Find the sum of the interior angle measures of the polygon.

Answers

1.

2.

1. _____

2. _____

3. _____

Find the measures of the interior angles of the polygon.

3.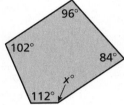

4.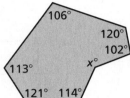

5.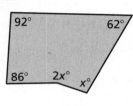

4. _____

5. _____

6. _____

7. _____

8. _____

Find the measures of the exterior angles of the polygon.

6.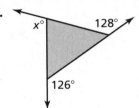

7.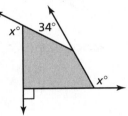

_____

_____

9. _____

_____

_____

Tell whether the triangles are similar. Explain.

8.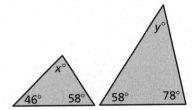

9.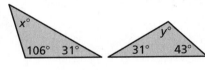

10. _____

11. a. _____

_____

_____

b. _____

10. The sum of the interior angle measures of a polygon is 5220°. How many sides does the polygon have?

11. You are trying to find the distance *d* across the river.

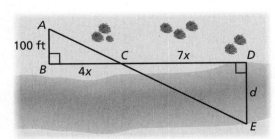

   a. Explain why △*ABC* and △*EDC* are similar.

   b. What is the distance across the river?

Chapter 3 **Test A**

Use the figure to find the measure of the angle. Explain your reasoning.

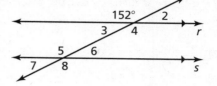

1. ∠4

2. ∠5

3. ∠8

4. ∠6

Find the measures of the interior angles.

5.

6.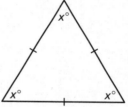

Find the measure of the exterior angle.

7.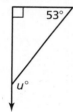

8.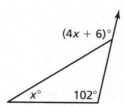

Find the measures of the interior angles of the polygon.

9.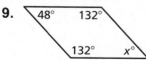

10.

Answers

1. _____

_____**See left.**_____

2. _____

_____**See left.**_____

3. _____

_____**See left.**_____

4. _____

_____**See left.**_____

5. _____

6. _____

7. _____

8. _____

9. _____

10. _____

Find the measures of the exterior angles of the polygon.

Answers

11.

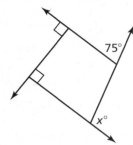

12.

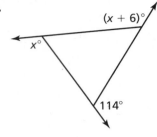

11. _____

_____

12. _____

_____

13. _____

_____

14. _____

_____

15. ___See left.___

16. _____

_____

17. _____

Tell whether the triangles are similar. Explain.

13.

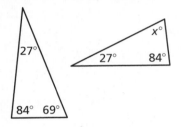

14.

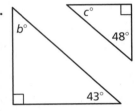

15. Describe two ways you can find the measure of ∠7.

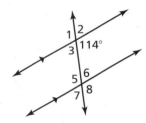

16. Can a hexagon have angles that measure 85°, 62°, 135°, 95°, 173°, and 160°? Explain.

17. You want to paddle a canoe across a small lake and want to know how far it is to the other side. You take measurements on your side of the lake and make the drawing shown. What is the distance x across the lake?

Chapter 3 Test B

Use the figure to find the measure of the angle. Explain your reasoning.

1. ∠6

2. ∠5

3. ∠4

4. ∠7

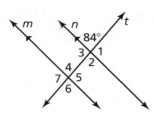

Answers

1. _____

   __See left.__

2. _____

   __See left.__

3. _____

   __See left.__

4. _____

   __See left.__

5. _____

6. _____

7. _____

8. _____

9. _____

10. _____

Find the measures of the interior angles.

5.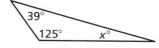

6.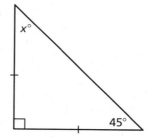

Find the measure of the exterior angle.

7.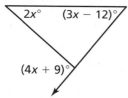

8.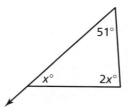

Find the sum of the interior angle measures of the polygon.

9.

10.

Chapter 3 **Test B** (continued)

Find the measures of the interior angles of the polygon.

Answers

11.

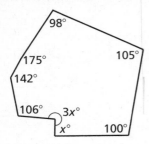

12.

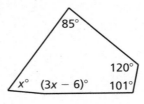

11. _____

_____

12. _____

_____

13. _____

Find the measures of the exterior angles of the polygon.

14. _____

13.

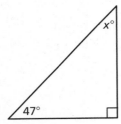

14.

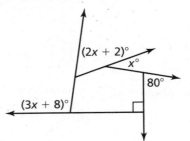

15. _____

_____

16. _____

17. _____

18. _____

15. Tell whether the triangles are similar. Explain.

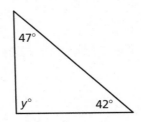

16. The measures of the acute angles of a right triangle have a ratio of 2 : 7. What is the measure of the smaller angle?

17. Five angles of a hexagon measures 150°, 82°, 127°, 99°, and 101°. Find the sixth angle measure.

18. You are on a boat in the ocean, at point *A*. You locate a lighthouse at point *D*, beyond the line of sight of the marker at point *C*. You travel 90 feet west to point *B* and then 36 feet south to point *C*. You travel 100 feet more to arrive at point *E*, which is due east of the lighthouse. What is the distance from point *E* to the lighthouse?

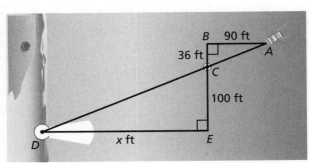

Chapter 3 Standards Assessment

1. What is the measure of ∠1?

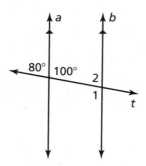

A. 80°

C. 100°

B. 90°

D. 180°

2. **GRIDDED RESPONSE** All of the angles in a regular octagon are congruent. What is the measure of each angle, in degrees?

3. The figures are similar.

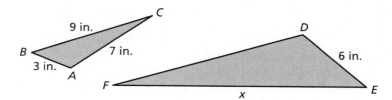

What is the value of x?

F. 2 inches

H. 14 inches

G. 7.7 inches

I. 18 inches

4. What value of x makes the equation below true?

$$\frac{x}{2} - 6 = -14$$

A. −40

C. −10

B. −16

D. −4

Chapter 3 Standards Assessment (continued)

5. Anita was solving the equation in the box below.

$$4x - 12 = 7x + 21$$
$$\underline{+\, 4x \qquad\qquad +\, 4x}$$
$$-12 = 11x + 21$$
$$\underline{-\, 21 \qquad\qquad -\, 21}$$
$$\frac{-33}{11} = \frac{11x}{11}$$
$$-3 = x$$

What should Anita do to correct the error that she made?

F. Subtract $4x$ from each side.

G. Add 21 to each side.

H. Multiply each side by 11.

I. Add $7x$ to each side.

6. The vertices of a triangle are $A(-4, 5)$, $B(-4, 1)$, $C(-1, 1)$. Rotate the triangle $180°$ about the origin. What are the coordinates of A'?

A. $(4, -5)$ **C.** $(-5, -4)$

B. $(5, 4)$ **D.** $(-5, 5)$

7. EXTENDED RESPONSE In the diagram shown, $\overline{AB}$ crosses $\overline{CD}$ at point X.

Part A   Explain how you can tell that $\triangle ACX$ is similar to $\triangle BDX$.

Part B   Suppose the measure of $\angle A$ is $35°$. List the measures of the remaining angles.

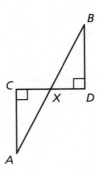

1. **A.** The student misinterprets the meaning of alternate interior and exterior angles.
   B. The student believes that $\angle 1$ is a right angle.
   C. Correct answer
   D. The student lists the sum of the measures of $\angle 1$ and $\angle 2$.

2. Correct answer: 135

   Common error: The student may think an octagon has six sides and write an answer of 120.

3. **F.** The student uses the wrong proportion to find the value of x.
   G. The student uses the wrong proportion to find the value of x.
   H. The student uses the wrong proportion to find the value of x.
   I. Correct answer

4. **A.** The student add -6 to both sides and then multiples both sides by 2.
   B. Correct answer
   C. The student adds -6 to both sides and then divides -20 by 2.
   D. The student adds 6 to both sides and then divides -8 by 2.

5. **F.** Correct answer
   G. The student forgets that the inverse operation of addition is subtraction.
   H. The student forgets that the inverse operation of multiplication is division.
   I. The student thinks that the variable must be on the left and uses the wrong operation.

6. **A.** Correct answer
   B. The student rotated the triangle 90° about the origin.
   C. The student rotated the triangle 270° about the origin.
   D. The student reflects the triangle in the y-axis.

7. **4 points** The student demonstrates a thorough understanding of how to use information in a diagram to show that triangles are similar and explains his or her thought process clearly. In Part A, the student makes clear that the two triangles have three pairs of corresponding congruent angles. (The angles formed at point X are congruent because they are vertical angles. Angles C and D are congruent because they are right angles. Angles A and B are congruent because they are the third angles in two triangles that already have two pairs of congruent angles.) Because all corresponding angles are congruent, $\triangle ACX$ is similar to $\triangle BDX$. In Part B, the student correctly indentifies the following angle measures: $\angle B = 35°$, $\angle C = 90°$, $\angle D = 90°$, and the measure of the angles formed at point X is $55°$.

3 points The student demonstrates an understanding of similar triangles and how to read a triangle diagram, but the student's work and explanations demonstrate an essential but less than thorough understanding.

2 points The student demonstrates a partial understanding of similar triangles and how to read a triangle diagram. He or she finds the congruent right angles and the congruent vertical angles but nothing more. A connection between congruent angles and similar triangles is not established.

1 point The student demonstrates a limited understanding of similar triangles and how to read a triangle diagram. The student's response is incomplete and exhibits many flaws.

0 points The student provides no response, a complete incorrect or incomprehensible response, or a response that demonstrates insufficient understanding of similar triangles and how to read a triangle diagram. The student finds, at most, one pair of congruent angles.

Alternative Assessment

ACEF is a rectangle. $\overline{AE}$ **is parallel to** $\overline{BD}$.

1. For each angle description, identify two pairs of angles and explain your reasoning.

   a. vertical angles

   b. corresponding angles

   c. supplementary angles

   d. complementary angles

   e. alternate interior angles

2. Find the measures of $\angle CFE$, $\angle AHC$, and $\angle CGD$. Explain how you found each measure.

3. Identify two pairs of similar triangles. Determine the side measures of those triangles. (Hint: Use ratios.)

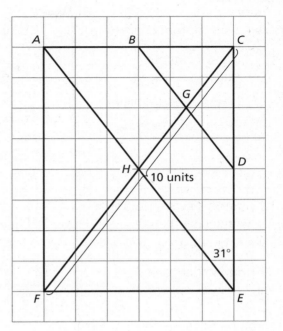

Chapter 3 Alternative Assessment Rubric

Score	Conceptual Understanding	Mathematical Skills	Work Habits
4	Shows complete understanding of: • angle relationships • similar triangles	Identifies two pairs of angles for all five types of angles. Correctly determines all angle measures and side lengths and justifies all answers.	Answers all questions. All work is neat and well organized.
3	Shows nearly complete understanding of: • angle relationships • similar triangles	Identifies one or two pairs of angles for three or four types of angles. Correctly determines two angle measures and most side lengths and justifies those answers.	Answers most questions. Most of the work is neat and well organized.
2	Shows some understanding of: • angle relationships • similar triangles	Identifies one pair of angles for two or three types of angles. Correctly determines one angle measure and one side length and justifies those answers.	Answers some questions. Some work is neat and organized.
1	Shows little understanding of: • identifying triangles by angles and sides • angle relationships • similar triangles	Does not identify pairs of angles for any type of angles. Does not determine any angle measures or side lengths and does not justify any answers.	Answers few questions. Work is sloppy and disorganized.

Name_____ Date_____

Graph the linear equation.

Answers

1. $y = \dfrac{1}{2}x - 3$

2. $y = -\dfrac{x}{4} + 1$

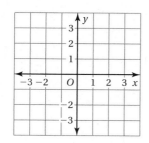

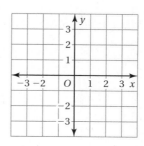

1. _____See left._____

2. _____See left._____

3. _____

4. _____

5. _____

6. _____See left._____

Find the slope of the line.

3.

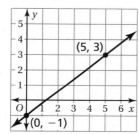

(5, 3)

(0, −1)

4.

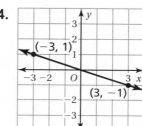

(−3, 1)

(3, −1)

7. a._____

b._____

5. What is the slope of a line that is perpendicular to the line in Exercise 3?

c. _____

6. The cost y (in dollars) for x pounds of deli meat is represented by the equation $y = 3.5x$. Graph the equation and interpret the slope.

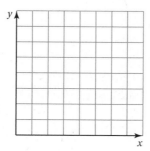

7. The amount y (in cups) of flour is proportional to the number x of eggs in a recipe. The recipe calls for 6 cups of flour for every 4 eggs.

  a. Write an equation that represents the situation.

  b. Interpret the slope.

  c. How many eggs are included when the recipe uses 12 cups of flour?

Chapter 4 **Quiz**
For use after Section 4.7

Find the slope and the *y*-intercept of the graph of the linear equation.

Answers

1. $y = -4x - 6$

2. $y = \dfrac{1}{2}x - \dfrac{1}{3}$

Find the *x*- and *y*-intercepts of the graph of the equation.

3. $3x - 4y = 24$

4. $-6x + 3y = 12$

5. You spend $40 on a meal for you and your friends.

  a. Graph the equation $2y + 5x = 40$, where x is the number of sandwiches purchased and y is the number of beverages purchased.

  b. Interpret the intercepts.

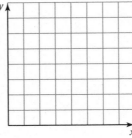

Write an equation of the line in slope-intercept form.

6.
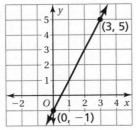

7.
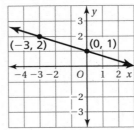

Write in point-slope form an equation of the line that passes through the given point and has the given slope.

8. $(1, 2);\ m = -2$

9. $(4, -2);\ m = \dfrac{1}{4}$

Write in slope-intercept form an equation of the line that passes through the given points.

10. $(-3, -1),\ (4, -1)$

11. $(2, 5),\ (0, 1)$

12. You are draining your fish aquarium. After 2 minutes, there are 6 gallons of water in the aquarium. After 5 minutes, the aquarium is empty. Write an equation that represents the volume y (in gallons) of water in the aquarium after x minutes.

1. _____

  _____

2. _____

  _____

3. _____

  _____

4. _____

  _____

5. a. ___See left.___

  b. _____

  _____

  _____

  _____

6. _____

7. _____

8. _____

9. _____

10. _____

11. _____

12. _____

Name_____ Date_____

Complete the table. Plot the two solution points and draw a line *exactly* through the two points. Find a different solution point on the line. (Use the same axes for both graphs.)

Answers

1.
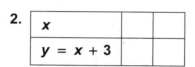

x		
$y = \dfrac{1}{2}x$		

2.

x		
$y = x + 3$		

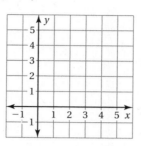

1. _____See left._____

_____

2. _____See left._____

_____

3. _____

4. _____

5. _____

Solve for *y*.

6. _____

3. $x + 4y = -12$

4. $2x - 3y = 3$

7. _____

Find the slope of the line.

5.
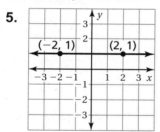

6.
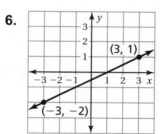

8. _____

9. _____

10. _____

7. Which is steeper, a slide that rises 3 feet for every 2 feet of run, or a sliding pole that rises 5 feet for every 3 feet of run? Explain.

11. _____

8. The equation of a line is $y = 2x - 3$. Write the equation of a line parallel to this line.

Find the slope and the *y*-intercept of the graph of the linear equation.

12. _____

9. $y = 3x - 6$ 10. $y + 5 = -\dfrac{3}{4}x$ 11. $y = \dfrac{7}{9}x - 3\dfrac{1}{3}$

12. The position *y* (in meters) of a submarine after *x* minutes is $y = -8x - 12$. Interpret the *y*-intercept and the slope.

Chapter 4 **Test A** (continued)

Graph the linear equation.

13. $-2x + 4y = 12$

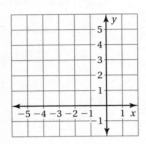

14. $2x + y = -4$

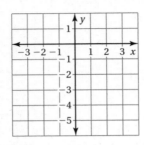

15. You are 9 miles away from home. You start biking home at a speed of 6 miles per hour.

   a. Write an equation in standard form that represents your distance from home y after x hours.

   b. Find the y-intercept of the graph. What does this represent?

   c. Find the x-intercept of the graph. What does this represent?

Write in slope-intercept form an equation of the line that passes through the given points.

16. $(0, 1), (2, 4)$

17. $(-3, 1), (0, 4)$

18. $(-3, 7), (2, -3)$

19. $(2, 8), (-2, 10)$

20. The graph shows the height y (in feet) of a kite x seconds after you start letting out the string.

   a. Find and interpret the slope of the graph.

   b. Write an equation of the line of the graph.

   c. What is the height of the kite after 15 seconds?

   d. Interpret the y-intercept of the graph.

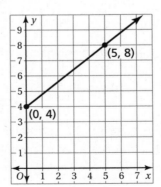

Answers

13. _____See left._____

14. _____See left._____

15. a._____

   b._____

   _____

   _____

   c._____

   _____

   _____

16. _____

17. _____

18. _____

19. _____

20. a.___See left.___

   b._____

   c._____

   d.___See left.___

Name_____ Date_____

Solve for *y*. Then graph the equation.

Answers

1. $3x + 2y = -4$

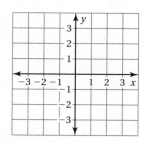

2. $4y - 3x = 4$

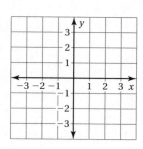

1. _____

_____See left._____

2. _____

_____See left._____

3. _____

4. _____

5. _____

Find the slope of the line.

3.

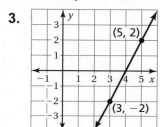

4.

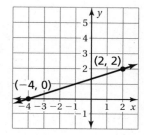

5. Which is steeper, a hill that rises 2 feet for every 10 feet of run, or a hill that rises 2 feet for every 15 feet of run? Explain.

6. Which two lines are parallel? Explain.

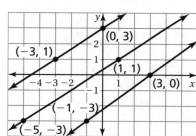

6. _____

7. _____

8. _____

9. _____

10. _____

Find the slope and the *y*-intercept of the graph of the linear equation.

7. $y = -2x - 1$ 　　**8.** $y - \dfrac{1}{3}x = 0$ 　　**9.** $y + 2 = \dfrac{3}{4}x$

10. Explain how to find the *x*-intercept of the graph of $y = 4x - 2$.

Chapter 4 Test B (continued)

Find the *x*-intercept and the *y*-intercept. Graph the equation.

11. $3x - 2y = 6$

12. $2x - y = -2$

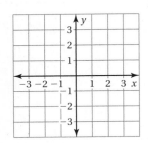

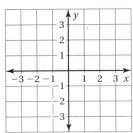

11. _____

_____

____See left.____

12. _____

_____

____See left.____

13. You borrow $90 from your grandmother. You pay back $15 each week.

   a. Write an equation in standard form that represents the amount owed *y* after *x* weeks.

   b. Find the *y*-intercept of the graph. What does this represent?

   c. Find the *x*-intercept of the graph. What does this represent?

13. a._____

b._____

_____

_____

c._____

_____

_____

Write in slope-intercept form an equation of the line that passes through the given points.

14. $(-3, -2), (0, 0)$

15. $(0, 3), (2, 3)$

16. $(-4, -3), (-2, 2)$

17. $(9, -5), (6, 4)$

14. _____

15. _____

16. _____

17. _____

18. The graph shows the relationship between temperature *y* (in degrees Fahrenheit) and altitude *x* (in thousands feet).

   a. Find and interpret the slope of the graph.

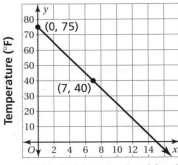

Altitude (thousands of feet)

   b. Write an equation of the line.

   c. Interpret the *x*-intercept of the graph.

18. .____See left.____

b._____

c.____See left.____

d._____

   d. What is the temperature at 11,000 feet?

Chapter 4 Standards Assessment

1. Carla plotted the points on the graph below to show how the amount she owes for tuition decreases as the number of tuition payments increases. The slope of the line segment joining these points is $-\dfrac{2}{3}$.

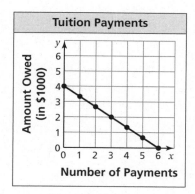

What does the slope of the line segment represent?

A. Each payment decreases the amount owed by $4,000.

B. Each payment decreases the amount owed by $0.66.

C. For every 3 payments, the amount owed decreases by $2,000.

D. For every 2 payments, the amount owed decreases by $3,000.

2. **GRIDDED RESPONSE** What value of k makes the equation below true?

$$5k - 12 = 22$$

3. A line contains the points $(0, 9)$ and $(6, 6)$. Which point is also on this line?

F. $(2, 5)$ **H.** $(-8, 5)$

G. $(4, 7)$ **I.** $(4, 4)$

4. Chris borrowed money from her brother. Each week she pays him $5 toward her debt. After 8 weeks, she has $8 left to pay. This situation is modeled by a line with a slope of -5 that contains the point $(9, 3)$. At what point does this line pass through the y-axis?

A. $(0, 45)$ **C.** $(0, -42)$

B. $(0, 24)$ **D.** $(0, 48)$

Chapter 4 **Standards Assessment** (continued)

5. Vivian charges $4 for bracelets and $5 for earrings. Her cost to make *x* bracelets and *y* earrings is $60. The equation $4x + 5y = 60$ represents this situation. The graph of this equation is a line. What is the slope of the line?

   F. -4 **H.** 0.8

   G. -0.8 **I.** 12

6. The math teacher asked Edith, "How old are you?" "Sixty years less than five times my brother's age," she answered. "That doesn't help me," replied the teacher. "Yes, it does," said Edith, "He and I are twins!" How old is Edith?

   A. 10 **C.** 15

   B. 12 **D.** 55

7. A line passes through the point $(1, 3)$ and has a slope of 2. Which of these points also lies on this line?

   F. $(1, 5)$ **H.** $(3, 5)$

   G. $(2, 6)$ **I.** $(3, 7)$

8. **SHORT RESPONSE** A car is traveling at a speed of 45 miles per hour. Once the car starts to brake, its speed (*s*) is related to the number of seconds (*t*) it spends braking according to the formula shown below.

$$s = -10t + 45$$

   Part A   Draw and label a graph that represents this situation on the coordinate grid below.

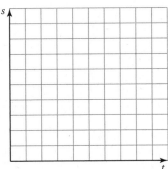

   Part B   Determine how many seconds it takes for the car to stop.

   Time to stop _____ seconds

1. **A.** The student mistakes the y-intercept for the slope.

   B. The student realizes the slope is $-\dfrac{2}{3}$, but doesn't realize the y-axis is in 1,000s, so each payment decreases the amount owed by \$666.67.

   C. Correct answer

   D. The student confuses the rise and run in the slope.

2. Correct answer: 6.8

   Common error: The student subtracts 12 from the right hand side instead of adding, leading to an incorrect answer of $k = 2$.

3. **F.** The student miscalculates the slope to be -2 and gets the equation $y = -2x + 9$.

   G. Correct answer

   H. The student miscalculates the slope to be $\dfrac{1}{2}$ and gets the equation

   $$y = \dfrac{1}{2}x + 9.$$

   I. The student correctly calculates the slope to be $-\dfrac{1}{2}$, but uses 6 for the

   y-intercept and gets the equation $y = -\dfrac{1}{2}x + 6$.

4. **A.** The student lets $y_1 = 0$ in the equation $y - y_1 = m(x - x_1)$.

   B. The student switches x_1 and y_1 in the equation $y - y_1 = m(x - x_1)$.

   C. The student lets $m = 5$ in the equation $y - y_1 = m(x - x_1)$.

   D. Correct answer

5. **F.** The student correctly subtracts $4x$ from each side but then fails to divide each side by 5.

   G. Correct answer

   H. The student divides 4 by 5 correctly but misplaces the minus sign, possibly by moving $4x$ to the right side incorrectly.

   I. The student divides 60 by 5, getting the y-intercept instead of the slope.

6. **A.** The student writes and solves the incorrect equation $60 - 5x = x$.

   B. The student writes the correct equation $5x - 60 = x$, but makes a mistake subtracting $5x$ and x, yielding $5x$ (because of the hidden coefficient on x) instead of $4x$.

   C. Correct answer

   D. The student misunderstands the problem and simply finds the difference between 60 and 5.

7. **F.** The student adds 2 to the *y*-coordinate to get another point because the slope is 2.

   G. The student multiplies both coordinates by 2 to get another point because the slope is 2.

   H. The student adds 2 to both coordinates to get another point because the slope is 2.

   I. Correct answer

8. **2 points** The student demonstrates a thorough understanding of translating a situation into a graph and then using the graph (or its related equation) to find the coordinates of a point on that graph. The graph is clearly labeled, properly scaled, and accurately drawn, showing a line from (0, 45) to (4.5, 0). The car stops after 4.5 seconds, and the student indicates this.

   1 point The student's work demonstrates limited understanding of translating a situation into a graph and then using the graph (or its related equation) to find the coordinates of a point on that graph. Either the graph is drawn incorrectly or the student cannot identify the correct point in Part B from a properly drawn graph.

   0 points The student provides no response, a completely incorrect or incomprehensible response, or a response that demonstrates insufficient understanding of making and interpreting graphs.

Name_____ Date _____

1. Sophia is going to make a tomato and fresh mozzarella cheese salad for a party. When she went to the farmer's market, she saw that the tomatoes she wanted were $2.50 per pound and that the fresh mozzarella cheese was $5.00 per pound. She is wondering what combinations of whole pounds of tomatoes and mozzarella cheese she can buy with $20.

   a. Write an equation that represents the pounds t of tomatoes and pounds m of mozzarella cheese she can buy with $20.

   b. Graph the equation. Interpret the intercepts.

   c. What combinations of whole pounds of the two ingredients can Sophia buy?

   d. Her recipe uses half as much mozzarella cheese as tomatoes. How much of each ingredient did she buy?

2. The graph shows the height of a Willow Oak Tree.

   a. Find the slope of the line.

   b. Explain the meaning of the slope as a rate of change.

   c. Write an equation of the line.

   d. What is the height of the tree after 30 years?

   e. If the tree growth is constant, when will the tree reach its maximum height of 60 feet?

   f. How would the graph change if the tree grew at a rate of 2 feet per year?

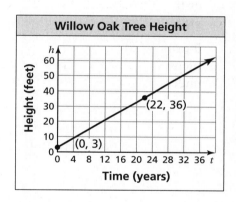

Willow Oak Tree Height

Chapter 4 — Alternative Assessment Rubric

Score	Conceptual Understanding	Mathematical Skills	Work Habits
4	Shows complete understanding of: • identifying slope, x-intercept, and y-intercept of equations graphically and algebraically • using an equation to represent a real-world situation	Writes and graphs the equation and interprets the graph to answer all of Exercise 1. Find the slope, writes the equation, and interprets the graph to answer all of Exercise 2.	Answers all parts of both problems. All equations and graph are written or drawn carefully and systematically. Work is very neat and well organized.
3	Shows nearly complete understanding of: • identifying slope, x-intercept, and y-intercept of equations graphically and algebraically • using an equation to represent a real-world situation	Writes and graphs the equation and interprets the graph to answer most of Exercise 1. Find the slope, writes the equation, and interprets the graph to answer most of Exercise 2.	Answers several parts of both problems. Most equations and graph are written or drawn carefully and systematically. Work is neat and organized.
2	Shows some understanding of: • identifying slope, x-intercept, and y-intercept of equations graphically and algebraically • using an equation to represent a real-world situation	Writes and graphs the equation and interprets the graph to answer some of Exercise 1. Find the slope, writes the equation, and interprets the graph to answer some of Exercise 2.	Answers some parts of both problems. Equations and graph are written or drawn carelessly. Work is not very neat or organized.
1	Shows little understanding of: • identifying slope, x-intercept, and y-intercept of equations graphically and algebraically • using an equation to represent a real-world situation	Does not write and graph the equation or interpret the graph to answer Exercise 1. Does not find the slope, write the equation, or interpret the graph to answer Exercise 2.	Does not attempt any part of either problem. No equations or graphs are written or drawn. Work is sloppy and disorganized.

Name_____ Date_____

Match the system of linear equations with the corresponding graph.
Use the graph to estimate the solution. Check your solution.

Answers

1. $y = x + 1$

$y = 2x - 1$

2. $y = -x - 1$

$y = -2x + 1$

A.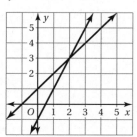

B.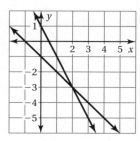

1. _____

_____

2. _____

_____

3. ___See left.___

_____

4. ___See left.___

_____

Solve the system of linear equations by graphing.

3. $y = -x - 2$

$y = \dfrac{1}{4}x + 3$

4. $-x + 2y = 2$

$-3x + 4y = 8$

5. _____

6. _____

7. _____

8. _____

9. _____

_____

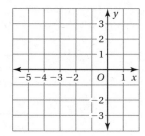

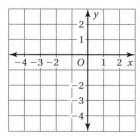

Solve the system of linear equations by substitution. Check your
solution.

5. $y = 2x + 3$

$y = 3x + 5$

6. $2x + y = 4$

$-3x + y = -1$

7. $y = \dfrac{1}{3}x + 2$

$y = \dfrac{1}{6}x + 4$

8. A math club has 40 members. The number of girls is 5 less than 2 times
the number of boys. How many members are boys? How many
members are girls?

9. The perimeter of a rectangle is 36 feet. The length is 2 less than 3 times
the width. What is the length? What is the width?

Name _____ Date _____

Solve the system of linear equations by elimination. Check your solution.

1. $x + 4y = 4$

$-x + 2y = 8$

2. $y = -9x + 2$

$y = -3x - 4$

3. $x + 6y = 12$

$x + 3y = 3$

Solve the system of linear equations. Check your solution.

4. $-6x + 3y = 9$

$-8x + 4y = 12$

5. $2x - 3y = 1$

$-4x + 6y = -4$

6. $-10x + 5y = 30$

$-2x + 2y = 6$

Use a graph to solve the equation. Check your solution.

7. $-2x + 3 = 4x - 3$

8. $-3x + 3 = -2x + 1$

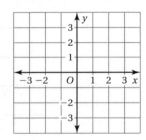

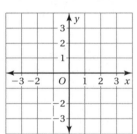

9. The table shows the purchases made by two customers at a meat counter. You want to buy 2 pounds of sliced ham and 3 pounds of sliced turkey. Can you determine how much you will pay? Explain.

	Sliced Turkey (pounds)	Sliced Ham (pounds)	Total Cost
Customer 1	0.5	1	$8.50
Customer 2	2	4	$34

10. A candle shop sells scented candles for $16 each and unscented candles for $10 each. The shop sells 28 candles today and makes $400.

a. Write a system of linear equations that represents the situation.

b. How many scented candles did the shop sell today? How many unscented candles did the shop sell today?

Answers

1. _____

2. _____

3. _____

4. _____

5. _____

6. _____

7. ____See left.____

_____

8. ____See left.____

_____

9. _____

_____

_____

_____

10. a._____

_____

b._____

_____

Chapter 5 Test A

Match the system of linear equations with the corresponding graph. Use the graph to estimate the solution. Check your solution.

Answers

1. $y = 3x - 2$

$y = 4x - 3$

2. $y = -2x - 3$

$y = 3x + 2$

A.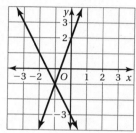

B.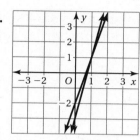

Solve the system of linear equations by graphing.

3. $y = -2x + 1$

$y = 2x - 3$

4. $y = 6x - 3$

$y = 4x - 1$

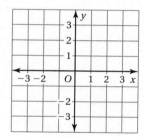

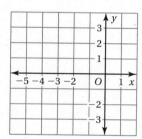

1. _____

_____

2. _____

_____

3. ___See left.___

_____

4. ___See left.___

_____

5. _____

6. _____

7. _____

8. _____

_____

9. _____

_____

Solve the system of linear equations by substitution. Check your solution.

5. $y = x + 2$

$y = 3x - 4$

6. $y = 3x + 4$

$x + y = 8$

7. $-2x + 3y = 9$

$y = 2x + 7$

8. There are 27 red or blue marbles in a bag. The number of red marbles is 5 less than 3 times the number of blue marbles. How many red marbles are in the bag? How many blue marbles are in the bag?

9. A fruit vendor sells 60 pieces of fruit that are either apples or oranges. The ratio of apples to oranges is 3 : 2. How many apples did the vendor sell? How many oranges did the vendor sell?

Chapter 5 **Test A** (continued)

Solve the system of linear equations by elimination. Check your solution.

Answers

10. $y = 5x - 8$
$y = -6x + 3$

11. $2x + 10y = -20$
$-x + 4y = 28$

12. $-x + 5y = 20$
$12y = 2x + 60$

10. _____

11. _____

12. _____

Without graphing, determine whether the system of linear equations has *one solution*, *infinitely many solutions*, or *no solution*. Explain your reasoning.

13. _____

13. $y = 4x + 6$
$2y = 8x + 12$

14. $y = 3x + 5$
$y = 3x - 5$

15. $y = 2x + 7$
$y = 3x - 1$

_____

_____

_____

14. _____

Use a graph to solve the equation. Check your solution.

16. $2x + 3 = 4x + 5$

17. $-3x - 3 = 2x + 2$

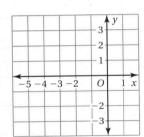

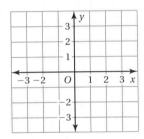

_____

_____

15. _____

_____

_____

16. ___See left.___

18. $3x + 1 = 3x + 2$

19. $\frac{1}{3}x + 1 = -\frac{2}{3}x + 2$

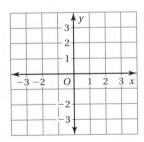

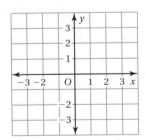

_____

17. ___See left.___

_____

18. ___See left.___

_____

19. ___See left.___

_____

20. At a sporting event, the price for 3 cheeseburgers and 2 cups of lemonade is $14 and the price for 2 cheeseburgers and 4 cups of lemonade is $12. How much does it cost for 1 cheeseburger and 2 cups of lemonade?

20. _____

21. _____

21. At a restaurant, you eat 2 taco salads and drink 2 glasses of iced tea. Your friend eats 1 taco salad and drinks 1 glass of iced tea. The restaurant charges you $11 and your friend $6.50. Can you determine the prices of taco salads and iced tea? Explain.

_____

_____

56 **Big Ideas Math Blue**
Assessment Book

Name_____ Date_____

Solve the system of linear equations by graphing.

Answers

1. $y = x + 3$

$y = -x - 3$

2. $y = \dfrac{1}{3}x + 2$

$y = 2x - 3$

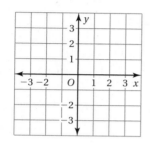

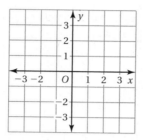

3. $y = 6x - 5$

$y = 5x - 4$

4. $x + 3y = 6$

$4x - 6y = 6$

1. ____See left.____

2. ____See left.____

3. ____See left.____

4. ____See left.____

5. _____

6. _____

7. _____

8. _____

9. _____

10. _____

Solve the system of linear equations by substitution. Check your solution.

5. $y = x + 3$

$y = 4x - 6$

6. $x + y = 7$

$y = 2x + 4$

7. $x - 3y = -12$

$y = 2x + 9$

8. There are 24 pens in a desk drawer. The pens are either red or blue. The ratio of red pens to blue pens is 5 : 1. How many pens are red? How many pens are blue?

9. There are 31 fish in a tank. The fish are either orange or red. There are 7 more orange fish than half the number of red fish. How many fish are orange? How many fish are red?

10. The measure of $\angle 1$ is 30 degrees less than twice the measure of $\angle 2$. What is the measure of $\angle 1$? What is the measure of $\angle 2$?

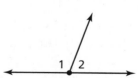

Chapter 5 **Test B** (continued)

Solve the system of linear equations by elimination. Check your solution.

Answers

11. $3x - y = 2$
$2x - y = 3$

12. $2x - y = -2$
$x - 2y = -16$

13. $6x - 2y = 10$
$10x - y = -2$

11. _____

12. _____

13. _____

Without graphing, determine whether the system of linear equations has *one solution*, *infinitely many solutions*, or *no solution*. Explain your reasoning.

14. _____

14. $y = 11x + 8$
$y = 9x - 7$

15. $14y = x + 6$
$28y = 2x + 12$

16. $y = 15x + 1$
$y = 15x + 2$

_____

_____

15. _____

Use a graph to solve the equation. Check your solution.

_____

17. $-2x - 1 = -x - 3$

18. $3x + 1 = 4x + 2$

_____

16. _____

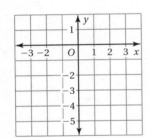

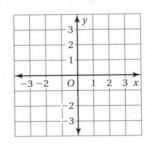

_____

_____

17. ___See left.___

19. $1 - 2x = -2x + 1$

20. $-\dfrac{1}{2}x - 2 = \dfrac{3}{2}x + 1$

_____

18. ___See left.___

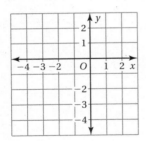

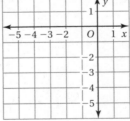

19. ___See left.___

_____

20. ___See left.___

_____

21. _____

21. One week you spent $24 on 6 subway tickets and 4 express bus tickets. The next week you spent $27 on 3 subway tickets and 7 express bus tickets. How much will it cost you to buy 5 subway tickets and 2 express bus tickets this week?

22. _____

_____

22. The weight of 3 identical containers holding a total of 9 gallons of fertilizer is 70.8 pounds. The weight of 5 of the containers holding a total of 15 gallons of fertilizer is 118.0 pounds. Can you determine the weight of each container? Explain.

_____

Chapter 5 Standards Assessment

1. What is the solution to the equation below?

$$-2x - 4 = -16$$

   A. -10 **C.** 6

   B. -6 **D.** 10

2. **GRIDDED RESPONSE** A middle school conducts a fire drill. The percent y (in decimal form) of students still inside x minutes after the fire alarm sounds is $y = -0.125x + 1$. After how many minutes are 75% of the students still inside?

3. The steps Andre took to solve the system of linear equations $y = 4x + 1$ and $y = 2x + 7$ are shown below. What should Andre change in order to correctly solve the system?

$$4x + 1 = 2x + 7$$
$$6x = 6$$
$$x = 1$$

   F. The constants should combine to equal 8.

   G. The x-terms should combine to equal $2x$.

   H. The constants should combine to equal 2.

   I. The x-terms should combine to equal $-6x$.

4. The formula for average acceleration over a period of time is $A = \dfrac{v_f - v_0}{t}$. How can this formula be solved for final velocity v_f?

   A. Multiply both sides of the formula by t.

   B. Add v_0 to both sides of the formula.

   C. Subtract t from both sides of the formula, then add v_0 to both sides of the formula.

   D. Multiply both sides of the formula by t, then add v_0 to both sides of the formula.

Chapter 5 Standards Assessment (continued)

5. Which ordered pair is a solution to the system of linear equations below?

$$y = \frac{1}{4}x + 2$$

$$y = x - 1$$

F. $(-4, 1)$ **H.** $(4, 3)$

G. $(3, 4)$ **I.** $(6, 4)$

6. The town library is having a used book sale. The graph to the right can be used to find the total cost y to buy x books. The total cost includes the admission fee.

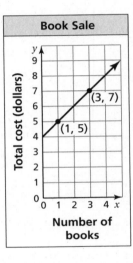

What is the equation of the line shown?

A. $y = x + 4$ **C.** $y = -x + 4$

B. $y = x - 4$ **D.** $y = -x - 4$

7. **EXTENDED RESPONSE** James and Max are saving their allowances to buy laptop computers. James has saved $30 already and earns a $5 allowance each week. Max has saved $10 already and earns a $10 allowance each week.

Part A   Write a system of equations that can represent this situation. Use x to represent the number of weeks and y to represent the total amount saved.

Equation for James _____

Equation for Max _____

Part B   After how many more weeks will James and Max have the same amount of money saved? Use your equations from Part A and the coordinate grid. Check your solution by solving the system using elimination or substitution.

Number of weeks _____

1. **A.** The student subtracts 4 from each side instead of adding 4, then divides each side by 2 instead of dividing by -2.

   B. The student divides each side by 2 instead of dividing by -2.

   C. Correct answer

   D. The student subtracts 4 from each side instead of adding 4.

2. Correct answer: 2

   Common error: The student adds 1 to the right side of the equation $-0.125x + 1 = 0.75$ instead of subtracting, leading to an incorrect answer of $x = -14$, which the student may change to 14.

3. **F.** The student adds 1 to each side, instead of subtracting 1.

   G. Correct answer

   H. The student divides each term by 4, but adds $\frac{1}{4}$ to each side instead of subtracting $\frac{1}{4}$.

   I. The student misapplies the sign rules of addition, thinking that 2 minus 4 equals -6.

4. **A.** The student takes one correct step then fails to completely solve for v_f.

   B. The student misunderstands what it means to solve for v_f and thinks $\frac{v_f - v_0}{t}$ can be separated using addition instead of multiplication.

   C. The student thinks $\frac{v_f - v_0}{t}$ can be separated using subtraction instead of multiplication.

   D. Correct answer

5. **F.** The ordered pair is a solution to the equation $y = \frac{1}{4}x + 2$, but not the other equation.

   G. The student switched the x- and y-coordinates when stating the solution.

   H. Correct answer

   I. The ordered pair is not a solution to either equation.

6. A. Correct answer

  B. The student gets the correct slope but the wrong y-intercept. The student is not taking the information available from the graph and is making a sign error during arithmetic.

  C. The student gets the wrong slope but the correct y-intercept. The student is not taking the information available from the graph and is making a sign error during arithmetic.

  D. The student gets the wrong slope and the wrong y-intercept. The student is not taking the information available from the graph and is making a sign error during arithmetic.

7. 4 points The student demonstrates a thorough understanding of setting up systems of equations and solving them by graphing. In Part A, the student writes the equations $y = 30 + 5x$ and $y = 10 + 10x$. In Part B, the student draws accurate graphs and obtains an answer of 4 weeks. The student also correctly checks the solution using elimination or substitution.

3 points The student demonstrates an understanding of setting up and solving systems of equations, but the student's work demonstrates an essential but less than thorough understanding.

2 points The student demonstrates a partial understanding of setting up and solving systems of equations. For example the graph of the system of equations is drawn incorrectly, or the student cannot check the solution using elimination or substitution.

1 point The student demonstrates limited understanding of setting up and solving systems of equations. For example, the system of equations has an error, the graph is drawn incorrectly, or the student cannot identify the correct point in Part B from a properly drawn graph.

0 points The student provided no response, a completely incorrect or incomprehensible response, or a response that demonstrates insufficient understanding of setting up and solving systems of equations.

Chapter 5 Alternative Assessment

1. The equations $y = x + 4$ and $4y = -3x + 44$ are part of a system of linear equations that have one solution.

   a. Graph the equations to find the solution to this system of linear equations.

   b. Draw a line that represents another equation that is part of this system of linear equations and has the same solution. Let the y-intercept of this line be 0. Explain how you drew this line.

   c. Write the equation of the line you drew in part (b).

   d. Write two other equations that have the same solution and are in this system of linear equations. Graph these equations to show that they intersect at the same point as the others.

   e. Show algebraically that all five equations you have written are satisfied by the common solution.

   f. Choose two of the equations that are part of this system of linear equations and write a problem that can be solved with the two equations.

2. Consider the equations $y = 2x - 4$ and $5y = 3x + 15$.

   a. Explain why these equations form a system of linear equations.

   b. Solve the system of linear equations graphically and algebraically. Show your steps.

   c. Find the slope of each equation. Explain how the slope can be determined from the equation and from the graph of the equation.

   d. Identify the x- and y-intercept of each equation. Explain how they can be found algebraically and graphically.

   e. Rewrite each equation in standard form.

Chapter 5 — Alternative Assessment Rubric

Score	Conceptual Understanding	Mathematical Skills	Work Habits
4	Shows complete understanding of: • solving systems of linear equations graphically and algebraically • identifying slope, x-intercept, and y-intercept of equations graphically and algebraically	Writes and graphs equation and interprets graph to answer all of Exercise 1. Correctly solves the system of linear equations graphically and algebraically. Identifies all features of both equations and rewrites both in standard form.	Answers all parts of both problems. All equations and graphs are written or drawn carefully and systematically. Work is very neat and well organized.
3	Shows nearly complete understanding of: • solving systems of linear equations graphically and algebraically • identifying slope, x-intercept, and y-intercept of equations graphically and algebraically	Writes and graphs equation and interprets graph to answer most of Exercise 1. Correctly solves the system of linear equations graphically or algebraically. Identifies some features of both equations and rewrites both in standard form.	Answers several parts of both problems. Most equations and graphs are written or drawn carefully and systematically. Work is neat and organized.
2	Shows some understanding of: • solving systems of linear equations graphically and algebraically • identifying slope, x-intercept, and y-intercept of equations graphically and algebraically	Writes and graphs equation and interprets graph to answer some of Exercise 1. Attempts to solve the system of linear equations graphically or algebraically. Identifies some features of both equations and rewrites one in standard form.	Answers some parts of both problems. Equations and graphs are written or drawn carelessly. Work is not very neat or organized.
1	Shows little understanding of: • solving systems of linear equations graphically and algebraically • identifying slope, x-intercept, and y-intercept of equations graphically and algebraically	Does not answer Exercise 1. Does not solve the system of linear equations either graphically or algebraically. Identifies no features of either equation and does not rewrite either in standard form.	Does not attempt any part of either problem. No equations or graphs are written or drawn. Work is sloppy and disorganized.

Name_____ Date_____

List the ordered pairs shown in the mapping diagram. Then determine whether the relation is a function.

Answers

1. Input   Output

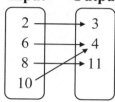

2. Input   Output

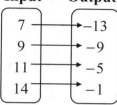

Find the value of *y* for the given value of *x*.

3. $y = \dfrac{1}{2}x$; $x = -18$

4. $y = -4x + 6$; $x = 1$

5. Write an equation that describes the function shown by the table.

Input, *x*	1	2	3	4
Output, *y*	-5	-10	-15	-20

Use the graph or table to write a linear function that relates *y* to *x*.

6.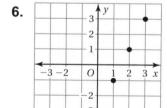

7.

x	–2	0	2	4
y	5	4	3	2

8. The table shows the amount of gasoline *g* (in gallons) left in your tank after you travel *m* miles.

   a. Write a linear function that relates the amount of gasoline to the traveling distance.

   b. How many gallons of gasoline are left after you drive 120 miles?

Miles, *m*	Gallons, *g*
0	20
20	19
40	18
60	17

Answers

1._____

_____

2._____

_____

3._____

4._____

5._____

6._____

7._____

8. a._____

   b._____

Name _____ Date _____

Does the table or graph represent a *linear* or *nonlinear* function?
Explain.

Answers

1.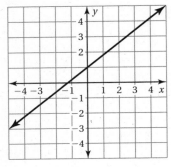

2.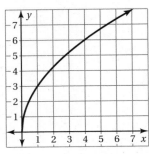

_____

2. _____

_____

3. _____

3.

Input, *x*	0	3	6	9
Output, *y*	1	4	7	10

4.

Input, *x*	4	8	12	16
Output, *y*	2	4	8	16

4. _____

_____

5. _____

Describe the relationship between the two quantities.

_____

5. Tickets

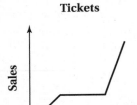

6. Bicycling

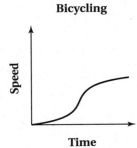

6. _____

_____

7. _____

7. Growth

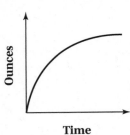

8. Account

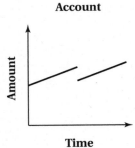

_____

8. _____

_____

9. _____

9. The table shows the value *v* (in thousands of dollars) of a house after *t* years. Does the table represent a linear or nonlinear function? Explain.

_____

Year, *t*	0	1	2	3
Value, *v*	105	110	116	120

Name_____ Date _____

List the ordered pairs shown in the mapping diagram.

1. Input   Output

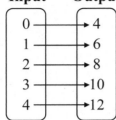

2. Input   Output

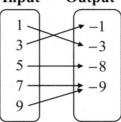

Answers

1. _____

_____

_____

_____

_____

2. _____

_____

_____

_____

_____

_____

Find the value of y for the given value of x.

3. $y = x - 5$; $x = 9$

4. $y = 4x$; $x = -7$

5. Write an equation that describes the function shown by the table.

Input, x	0	1	2	3	4
Output, y	0	5	10	15	20

6. Write a function rule for the statement, "The output is 4 less than the input." Then complete the table.

Input, x	1	2	3	4
Output, y				

3. _____

4. _____

5. _____

6. _____

_____See left._____

Use the graph or table to write a linear function that relates y to x.

7.

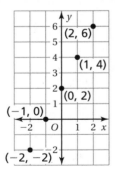

8.

x	-1	0	1	2
y	-4	0	4	8

7. _____

8. _____

Chapter 6 **Test A** (continued)

Graph the function.

Answers

9. $y = -2x + 1$

10. $y = \dfrac{1}{4}x$

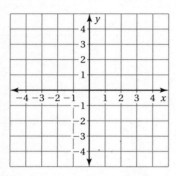

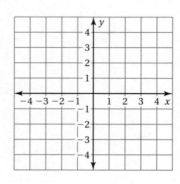

Does the table or graph represent a *linear* or *nonlinear* function? Explain.

11.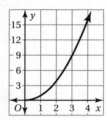

12.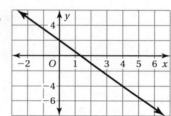

13.

Input, x	1	2	3	4
Output, y	0	3	8	15

14.

Input, x	1	2	3	4
Output, y	−1	−3	−5	−7

15. The table shows the number y of muffins baked in x pans. What is the missing y-value that makes the table represent a linear function?

Pans, x	3	4	5
Muffins, y	18	?	30

16. The graph shows the water usage for a business. Describe the change in usage from July to December.

9. _____See left._____

10. _____See left._____

11. _____

_____

_____

_____

12. _____

_____

_____

13. _____

_____

_____

_____

14. _____

_____

_____

15. _____

16. _____

_____

Name_____ Date_____

Test B

Draw a mapping diagram of the set of ordered pairs.

1. $(0, -8), (1, -6), (2, -4), (3, -2)$ **2.** $(3, 8), (4, 6), (5, 8), (6, 4)$

3. The table shows the speed of a falling parachutist.

Time (seconds)	0.1	0.2	0.3	0.4	0.5
Speed (meters per second)	0.9	1.9	2.9	3.9	4.9

  a. Use the table to draw a mapping diagram.

  b. What output would you expect for an input of 0.7 second? Explain.

Write a function rule for the statement.

4. The output is 2 less than the input.

5. The output is one third the input.

Find the value of *x* for the given value of *y*.

6. $y = 2x - 2; \ y = 14$ **7.** $y = 5x - 1; \ y = -6$

8. A clerk earns \$8 an hour. Write a function that relates the earnings E and hours worked h. How much does the clerk earn after working 40 hours?

Graph the function.

9. $y = -x$ **10.** $y = \dfrac{3}{2}x + 2$

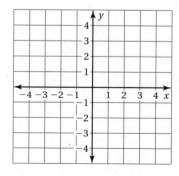

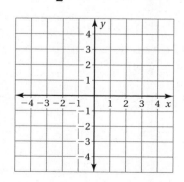

Answers

1. _____See left._____

2. _____See left._____

3. a._____See left._____

  b._____

  _____

  _____

4. _____

5. _____

6. _____

7. _____

8. _____

  _____

9. _____See left._____

10. _____See left._____

Chapter 6 **Test B** (continued)

Use the graph or table to write a linear function that relates *y* to *x*.

Answers

11.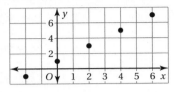

12.

x	−12	−6	0	6
y	6	3	0	−3

11. _____

12. _____

13. a. _____

13. You are packing candles in boxes. You can fit 15 candles in each box.

b. _____

  a. Write a function that represents the number of candles that you pack into *x* boxes.

14. _____

  b. How many boxes do you need to pack 75 candles?

15. _____

14. The table shows the values *y* (in dollars) of Car A and Car B after *x* years of ownership. Which function represents a linear function: the function for *Car A*, for *Car B*, for *both*, or for *neither of them*?

_____

16. _____

Years, x	0	1	2	3
Value of Car A, y	24,000	20,000	16,000	12,000
Value of Car B, y	24,000	12,000	6000	3000

_____

_____

17. _____

Does the equation represent a *linear* or *nonlinear* function? Explain.

18. a. _____

15. $y = \dfrac{2}{x} + 1$ **16.** $y + 7 = 2x + 3y$

_____

_____

17. The table shows the cost *y* (in dollars) for *x* theater tickets. Find the missing *y*-value that makes the table represent a linear function.

Tickets, x	2	4	6
Cost, y	26	?	78

_____

_____

18. An anthropologist uses the two functions below to estimate the height *h* of an individual given the length *t* of the thigh bone. Both measurements are in inches.

b. _____

  Male: $h = 2.2t + 27$ Female: $h = 2.3t + 24$

_____

  a. If you graphed the two functions, which one would rise more steeply? How do you know?

  b. Find the height of a male and of a female with a 15-inch thigh bone.

c. _____

  c. Find the length of the thigh bone of a 71-inch tall man.

Chapter 6 Standards Assessment

1. Which equation represents the function shown in the input-output table below?

Input, x	1	2	3	4
Output, y	10	17	24	31

    A. $y = 10x$ **C.** $y = 3x + 7$

    B. $y = 7x + 3$ **D.** $y = x + 9$

2. **GRIDDED RESPONSE** Dan returns $42.50 worth of merchandise and then buys 4 shirts for $7.84 each. How much money does Dan have left?

3. Which description is a correct way to solve the equation below?

$$\frac{x}{5} + 4.3 = 12.4$$

    F. Subtract 4.3 from both sides then divide both sides by 5.

    G. Add 4.3 to both sides then multiply both sides by 5.

    H. Subtract 4.3 from both sides then multiply both sides by 5.

    I. Add 4.3 to both sides then divide both sides by 5.

4. Which point appears on the graph of the function below?

    $y = 2x + 3$

    A. $(0, 0)$ **C.** $(3, 0)$

    B. $(0, 3)$ **D.** $(-3, 0)$

5. What is the value of w in the equation below when $z = 4$?

    $w = 12z - 9.7$

    F. 2.3   **H.** 57.7

    G. 38.3   **I.** 114.3

Chapter 6 Standards Assessment (continued)

6. Which method can you use to eliminate a variable from the following system of equations?

$$2x - 6y = 3$$
$$4x + y = -3$$

   A. Add the first equation to the second equation.

   B. Subtract the first equation from the second equation.

   C. Add twice the first equation to the second equation.

   D. Subtract twice the first equation from the second equation.

7. The vertices of a triangle $X(-4, 5)$, $Y(-4, 1)$, and $Z(-1, 1)$. Reflect the triangle in the y-axis. What are the coordinates of X'?

   F. $(4, 5)$ **H.** $(4, -5)$

   G. $(-4, -5)$ **I.** $(0, 5)$

8. The profit y from selling x muffins can be represented by a linear function. The profit from selling 5 muffins is $4. The profit from selling 7 muffins is $8. What is the slope of the line represented by the data?

   A. $\dfrac{1}{2}$ **C.** $\dfrac{4}{5}$

   B. 1 **D.** 2

9. **SHORT RESPONSE** To repair an air conditioner, David charges a one-time fee for a service call plus an hourly rate for the time required for the repair.

   Part A   Complete the input-output table below for the total amount y that David will charge for a repair that requires x hours.

Input, x	1	2	3	4	5	6
Output, y	120	165	210			

   Part B   What is the hourly rate that David charges? Explain your reasoning.

   Hourly rate $_____

1. **A.** The student uses only the first input and output and determines that the output is 10 times the input. This equation will not work for any other inputs and outputs.

   B. Correct answer

   C. The student reverses the 7 and the 3 from the correct equation, resulting in an equation that works for the first input and output but not for the rest.

   D. The student uses only the first input and output and determines that the output is 9 more than the input. This equation will not work for any other inputs and outputs.

2. Correct answer: $11.14

   Common error: The student adds the two amounts together instead of subtracting, getting $73.86.

3. **F.** The student divides instead of multiplies.

   G. The student adds instead of subtracts.

   H. Correct answer

   I. The student adds instead of subtracts and divides instead of multiplies.

4. **A.** The student assumes the origin must be part of the graph.

   B. Correct answer

   C. The student has confused the position of x and y in the ordered pair.

   D. The student assumes the -3 will cancel out the positive 3 and yield zero.

5. **F.** The student ignores the variable and subtracts 9.7 from 12.

   G. Correct answer

   H. The student adds 9.7 instead of subtracts.

   I. The student thinks that $12z$ means 124 and finds $124 - 9.7$.

6. **A.** The student forgets that equations need variables with opposite coefficients to eliminate by addition or the student eliminates the constant instead of a variable.

   B. The student forgets that equations need variables with equal coefficients to eliminate by subtraction or incorrectly tries to eliminate the constant instead of a variable.

   C. The student forgets that equations need variables with opposite not equal coefficients to eliminate by addition.

   D. Correct answer

7. **F.** Correct answer
   G. The student reflects the triangle in the *x*-axis.
   H. The student reflects the triangle in the *x*-axis, then in the *y*-axis.
   I. The student translates the triangle 4 units to the right.

8. **A.** The student either found the change in *x* over the change in *y* or wrote the coordinates as (y, x).

   B. The student found the sum of the *y*-values over the sum of the *x*-values.

   C. The student only used the point $(5, 4)$ to find a slope of $\dfrac{y}{x}$.

   D. Correct answer

9. **2 points** The student demonstrates a thorough understanding of working with input-output tables and graphs of linear functions. In Part A, the student correctly completes the table with the following outputs, in order: 255, 300, 345. In Part B, the student correctly explains why the hourly rate is $45.

   1 point The student demonstrates a limited understanding of working with input-output tables and graphs of linear functions. The student's response is incomplete and exhibits many flaws.

   0 points The student provided no response, a completely incorrect or incomprehensible response, or a response that demonstrates insufficient understanding of working with input-output tables and graphs of linear functions.

Chapter 6 Alternative Assessment

1. Lou and Gene purchase new DVDs every week for 10 weeks. The input-output tables below show the total number of DVDs they each own.

Number of weeks, x	0	1	3	5	10
Lou's DVDs, y	10	12	16	20	30

Number of weeks, x	0	1	3	5	10
Gene's DVDs, y	2	5	11	17	32

a. Draw a mapping diagram for each person.

b. For each person, write an equation that describes the function shown by the table.

c. Use the equations in part (b) to determine how many DVDs they would each have if they continued the same pattern for ten additional weeks.

d. Graph both functions. Which graph is steeper? Explain.

e. What does the intersection of the two graphs represent?

f. After 15 weeks, Gene claims to have 46 DVDs, and Lou claims to have 40 DVDs. Use your equations in part (b) to explain whether or not each person is correct.

g. Sam's DVD purchases over the same 10 weeks are shown in an input-output table. Use the first three input values to write an equation for the function shown by the table. Then find the missing input.

Number of weeks, x	0	2	4	
Sam's DVDs, y	12	22	32	77

h. Create an input-output table and write an equation that represents a person starting with 20 DVDs and buying 4 new DVDs each week.

Chapter 6 Alternative Assessment Rubric

Score	Conceptual Understanding	Mathematical Skills	Work Habits
4	Shows complete understanding of: • finding and graphing a linear function of given data points • determining if an ordered pair is a solution • steepness and intersection of linear functions	Shows all work. Answers all questions correctly.	Answers all parts of each problem. Work is neat and well organized.
3	Shows nearly complete understanding of: • finding and graphing a linear function of given data points • determining if an ordered pair is a solution • steepness and intersection of linear functions	Shows most of the work. Makes one or two computational errors.	Answers all parts of each problem. Work is neat and easy to follow.
2	Shows some understanding of: • finding and graphing a linear function of given data points • determining if an ordered pair is a solution • steepness and intersection of linear functions	Shows some work. Makes more than two computational errors.	Answers all parts of each problem. Work is sloppy and hard to follow.
1	Shows little understanding of: • finding and graphing a linear function of given data points • determining if an ordered pair is a solution • steepness and intersection of linear functions	Shows very little or no work. Makes many computational errors.	Does not answer all parts of each problem. Work is sloppy and hard to follow.

Name_____ Date_____

Find the square root(s).

1. $-\sqrt{16}$

2. $\sqrt{\dfrac{25}{169}}$

3. $\pm\sqrt{12.25}$

Find the cube root.

4. $\sqrt[3]{512}$

5. $\sqrt[3]{-8}$

6. $\sqrt[3]{\dfrac{64}{27}}$

Evaluate the expression.

7. $5\sqrt{4} - \sqrt{49}$

8. $-4\sqrt{100} + 10\sqrt{16}$

9. $2\sqrt{\dfrac{25}{64}} - \dfrac{3}{8}$

10. $\left(\sqrt[3]{1000}\right)^3 + 6$

11. $5\sqrt[3]{-64} + 45$

12. $61 - 2\sqrt[3]{-125}$

Find the missing length of the triangle.

13.

14.

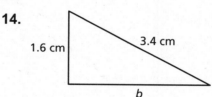

15.

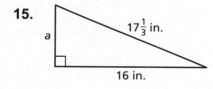

16.

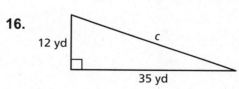

17. The value of the circumference of Circle A is three times the value of the area of Circle B. What is the radius of Circle B?

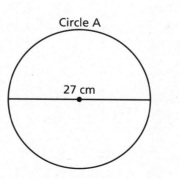

Circle A

27 cm

18. A cube-shaped box has a volume of 1331 cubic inches. How tall is the box?

Answers

1. _____

2. _____

3. _____

4. _____

5. _____

6. _____

7. _____

8. _____

9. _____

10. _____

11. _____

12. _____

13. _____

14. _____

15. _____

16. _____

17. _____

18. _____

Name _____ Date _____

Classify the real number.

Answers

1. $\sqrt{2}$ **2.** $\dfrac{1}{11}$ **3.** 7

1. _____

2. _____

Estimate the square root to the nearest (a) integer and (b) tenth.

3. _____

4. $\sqrt{24}$ **5.** $-\sqrt{220}$ **6.** $\sqrt{\dfrac{18}{5}}$

4. a._____

   b._____

5. a._____

Which number is greater? Explain.

   b._____

7. $\sqrt{\dfrac{1}{102}}, \dfrac{1}{9}$ **8.** $\pi, \sqrt{\pi}$

6. a._____

   b._____

Write the decimal as a fraction or a mixed number.

7. _____

9. $2.\overline{4}$ **10.** $-3.\overline{27}$

   _____

Tell whether the triangle with the given side lengths is a right triangle.

11. 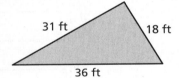   **12.**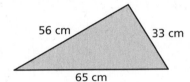

   _____

8. _____

   _____

Find the distance between the two points.

9. _____

10. _____

13. $(0, 0), (3, 4)$ **14.** $(2, -3), (7, -15)$

11. _____

15. $(-5, -1), (0, 2)$ **16.** $(-1, 4), (-3, -2)$

12. _____

13. _____

17. A car leaves a parking ramp and travels 5 miles due east. The car makes a 90° turn and travels 12 miles due north. The car has enough gas in the tank to travel 12.7 miles. Can the car make it back to the parking ramp using a direct route? Explain your reasoning.

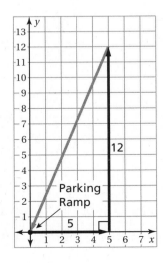

14. _____

15. _____

16. _____

17. _____

   _____

   _____

   _____

Name_____ Date _____

Test A

Find the square root(s).

1. $-\sqrt{81}$

2. $\pm\sqrt{\dfrac{1}{9}}$

Find the cube root.

3. $\sqrt[3]{-1}$

4. $\sqrt[3]{-\dfrac{8}{27}}$

Evaluate the expression.

5. $10 - 2\sqrt{9}$

6. $\sqrt{0.25} + 2.4$

7. $70 - \left(\sqrt[3]{64}\right)^3$

8. $5\sqrt[3]{-27} + 18$

9. The area of a square game court is 64 square feet. How long is one side of the court?

10. The ratio of the areas of the two squares is 25 to 9. The side length of the smaller square is 30 meters. How long is the side length of the larger square? Explain your reasoning.

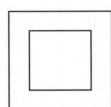

Find the missing length of the triangle.

11.

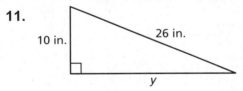

10 in.   26 in. y

12.

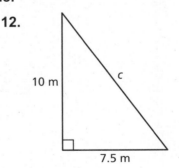

10 m c 7.5 m

13. A slide is 21 feet high, as shown. What is the length of the slide (the hypotenuse)?

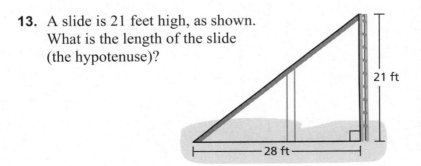

21 ft

28 ft

Answers

1. _____

2. _____

3. _____

4. _____

5. _____

6. _____

7. _____

8. _____

9. _____

10. _____

_____

_____

11. _____

12. _____

13. _____

Chapter 7 **Test A** (continued)

Classify the real number.

14. $-\sqrt{16}$ **15.** $\dfrac{3\pi}{2}$ **16.** $9.\overline{63}$

Estimate the square root to the nearest (a) integer and (b) tenth.

17. $\sqrt{37}$ **18.** $-\sqrt{52}$ **19.** $\sqrt{3.3}$

20. Find the perimeter of the trapezoidal brick to the nearest tenth of an inch.

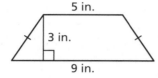

Which number is greater? Explain.

21. $\sqrt{17}$, 4.5   **22.** $-10\dfrac{1}{5}$, $-\sqrt{120}$

Write the decimal as a fraction or a mixed number.

23. $1.\overline{3}$ **24.** $0.\overline{14}$

Find the distance between the two points.

25. $(-3, 6)$, $(5, -9)$ **26.** $(-2, 7)$, $(3, -1)$

Tell whether the triangle with the given side lengths is a right triangle.

27.

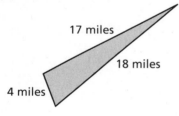

28.

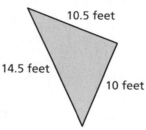

29. Find the distance d. Round your answer to the nearest tenth.

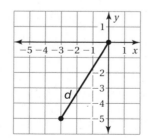

14. _____

15. _____

16. _____

17. a._____

b._____

18. a._____

b._____

19. a._____

b._____

20. _____

21. _____

_____

22. _____

_____

23. _____

24. _____

25. _____

26. _____

27. _____

28. _____

29. _____

Name_____ Date _____

Chapter 7 Test B

Find the square root(s).

Answers

1. $-\sqrt{169}$ **2.** $\pm\sqrt{10,000}$ **3.** $\sqrt{\dfrac{16}{81}}$

1. _____

2. _____

Find the cube root.

3. _____

4. $\sqrt[3]{1,000,000}$ **5.** $\sqrt[3]{\dfrac{27}{729}}$

4. _____

5. _____

Evaluate the expression.

6. _____

6. $3 - \sqrt{0.0225}$ **7.** $\sqrt{0.25} + \left(\sqrt{0.64}\right)^2$

7. _____

8. _____

8. $6\sqrt[3]{1331} - 42$ **9.** $3\sqrt[3]{-\dfrac{1}{64}} + 2\dfrac{1}{2}$

9. _____

10. A cube-shaped aquarium has a volume of 1728 cubic inches. What is the width of the aquarium?

10. _____

11. _____

Find the missing length of the triangle.

12. _____

11. **12.**

13. a. _____

b. _____

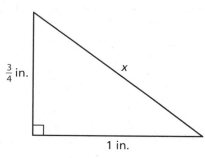

14. _____

15. _____

16. _____

13. A toy marble run has ramps and turnaround points. Each ramp is 41 centimeters long. The turnaround is 2 centimeters wide and flat, and the entire toy is 42 centimeters wide, as shown.

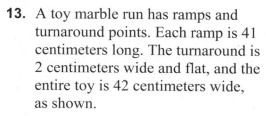

a. How tall is the toy?

b. You add one more ramp to the toy. How tall is it now?

Classify the real number.

14. $1\dfrac{5}{7}$ **15.** $-\sqrt{3}$ **16.** $\sqrt{\dfrac{1}{8}}$

Big Ideas Math Blue **81**
Assessment Book

Chapter 7 **Test B** (Continued)

Estimate the square root to the nearest (a) integer and (b) tenth.

17. $-\sqrt{46}$ **18.** $\sqrt{190}$

19. The time in seconds for an object to fall d meters is modeled by $\sqrt{\dfrac{d}{5}}$.
How long does it take the object to fall 200 meters? Round to the nearest tenth of a second.

Which number is greater? Explain.

20. $\sqrt{4.4}$, 2.2   **21.** $-\sqrt{0.8}$, -0.8

Write the decimal as a fraction or a mixed number.

22. $0.\overline{37}$ **23.** $7.\overline{18}$

Find the distance between the two points.

24. $(-10, 9)$, $(10, -12)$ **25.** $(10, -4)$, $(-14, 6)$

Tell whether the triangle with the given side lengths is a right triangle.

26. 8 ft, 15 ft, 17 ft   **27.** 14 km, 48 km, 50 km

28. Find the side lengths of the triangle in the figure. Is it a right triangle? Explain your reasoning.

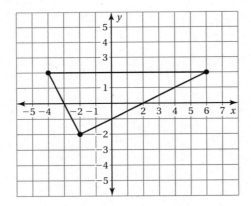

29. The diagonal of a square is 2 inches. Find the area of the square.

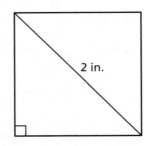

2 in.

Answers

17. a._____

    b._____

18. a._____

    b._____

19. _____

20. _____

_____

_____

21. _____

_____

_____

_____

22. _____

23. _____

24. _____

25. _____

26. _____

27. _____

28. _____

_____

_____

_____

_____

_____

_____

29. _____

Chapter 7 Standards Assessment

1. The graph shows the height of a plant *y*, measured in inches, after *x* weeks. Which linear function relates *y* to *x*?

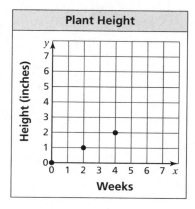

Plant Height

   A. $y = x - 1$ **C.** $y = x - 2$

   B. $y = \dfrac{1}{2}x$ **D.** $y = 2x$

2. **GRIDDED RESPONSE** The sum of the measures of the angles in a polygon is 900 degrees. How many sides does the polygon have?

3. The formula below can be used to find the surface area of a cone. Solve the formula for ℓ.

$$S = \pi r^2 + \pi r \ell$$

   F. $\ell = \pi r^2 + \pi r S$ **H.** $\ell = \dfrac{S - \pi r^2}{\pi r}$

   G. $\ell = \dfrac{S + \pi r^2}{\pi r}$ **I.** $\ell = \dfrac{S}{\pi r} - \pi r^2$

4. The steps Will took to simplify an expression are shown below. What should Will change in order to correctly simplify the expression?

$$\frac{9}{\sqrt{9}} = \frac{1}{\sqrt{1}} = 1$$

   A. The answer should be ±1.

   B. Simplify $\sqrt{9}$ first and then divide.

   C. Square the entire expression to remove the square root.

   D. Square just the denominator of the expression to remove the square root.

Chapter 7 **Standards Assessment** (continued)

5. The graph below shows the linear relationship between the number of game tickets x and the total cost y to attend a school fair.

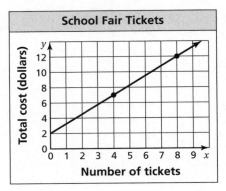

What is the slope of the line?

F. 2 **H.** 1

G. 1.25 **I.** 0.8

6. Between which two integers does $-\sqrt{41}$ lie?

A. 6 and 7 **C.** -7 and -8

B. -6 and -7 **D.** -20 and -21

7. **EXTENDED RESPONSE** In the diagram below, $AB = BC = CD = DE = 1$.

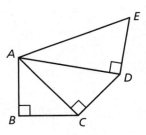

Part A What formula can you use to find AC?

_____

Part B Find AC, AD, and AE. Show your work clearly.

Part C Which lengths in the figure are irrational numbers? How can you tell?

1. **A.** The student misreads the graph and picks an equation that passes through the point (2, 1).

   B. Correct answer

   C. The student misreads the graph and picks an equation that passes through the point (4, 2).

   D. The student inverts the slope.

2. Correct answer: 7

   Common error: The student divides 900 by 180 and gets 5 as an answer.

3. **F.** The student switches the variables ℓ and S.

   G. The student adds πr^2 to each side instead of subtracting πr^2.

   H. Correct answer

   I. The student forgets to divide all terms by πr.

4. **A.** The student has applied the order of operations incorrectly.

   B. Correct answer

   C. The student has applied the properties of equality to an expression incorrectly.

   D. The student has applied the properties of equality to an expression incorrectly.

5. **F.** The student picks the y-intercept instead of the slope.

   G. Correct answer

   H. The student miscounts squares when calculating slope.

   I. The student reverses the roles of x and y in the slope formula.

6. **A.** The student overlooks the negative sign.

   B. Correct answer

   C. The student picks the adjacent interval.

   D. The student takes half of 41 as the square root.

7. **4 points** The student demonstrates a thorough understanding of the Pythagorean Theorem and how to apply it to a complicated diagram. Additionally, the student understands how to tell if a root is a rational number. Lengths obtained in the problem are $AC = \sqrt{2}$, $AD = \sqrt{3}$, and $AE = 2$.

3 points The student demonstrates an essential but less than thorough understanding of the Pythagorean Theorem and its application. A small error may be made in finding one of the lengths or in identifying a number as rational or irrational.

2 points The student's work and explanations demonstrate a lack of essential understanding of the Pythagorean Theorem and its application. The student makes numerous errors applying the theorem to the diagram.

1 point The student demonstrates limited understanding. The student's response is incomplete and exhibits many flaws.

0 points The student provides no response, a completely incorrect or incomprehensible response, or a response that demonstrates insufficient understanding of the Pythagorean Theorem and its application.

Chapter 7 Alternative Assessment

1. Use the expressions below.

$$\sqrt{90} \qquad \sqrt{909} \qquad \sqrt{9} \qquad \sqrt{900} \qquad \sqrt{9}\pi$$

    a. Evaluate each expression.

    b. Order the expressions from least to greatest.

    c. Tell whether each expression is *rational* or *irrational*. Explain.

2. $ABCD$ is a quadrilateral composed of two right triangles where $AD = 3$, $AB = AD + 1$, and $DC = AD \times AB$.

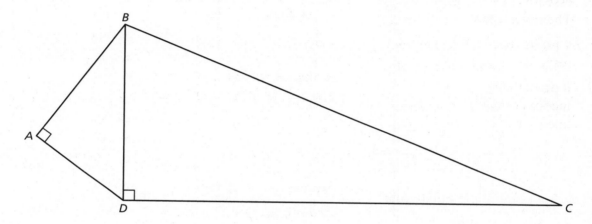

    a. Find AB, DC, BD, and BC.

    b. Is $\triangle BAD$ similar to $\triangle CDB$? Explain your reasoning.

Name _____ Date _____

Score	Conceptual Understanding	Mathematical Skills	Work Habits
4	Shows complete understanding of: • squares and square roots • rational and irrational numbers • the Pythagorean Theorem	Evaluated and ordered all expressions correctly. Determined all side lengths of the triangles and explained why the two triangles are not similar.	Answers all parts of all questions. All calculations are done carefully. All work is neat and well organized.
3	Shows nearly complete understanding of: • squares and square roots • rational and irrational numbers • the Pythagorean Theorem	Evaluated and ordered most expressions correctly. Determined some side lengths of the triangles and explained why the two triangles are not similar.	Answers almost all questions. Most of the calculations are done carefully. Most of the work is neat and well organized.
2	Shows some understanding of: • squares and square roots • rational and irrational numbers • the Pythagorean Theorem	Evaluated and ordered some expressions correctly. Determined few side lengths of the triangles and said that the two triangles are similar.	Answers some parts of all questions. Some calculations are done carefully. Some work is neat and well organized.
1	Shows little understanding of: • squares and square roots • rational and irrational numbers • the Pythagorean Theorem	Did not evaluate or order the expressions correctly. Did not determine side lengths of the triangles or explain why the two triangles are not similar.	Answers few parts of the questions. No calculations are done carefully. All work is sloppy and disorganized.

Chapter 8 **Quiz**
For use after Section 8.2

Find the volume of the solid. Round your answer to the nearest tenth.   *Answers*

1.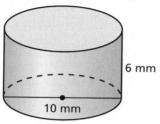
6 mm
10 mm

2.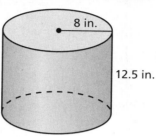
8 in.
12.5 in.

3.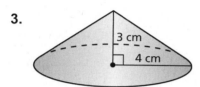
3 cm
4 cm

4.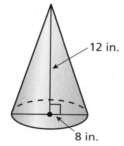
12 in.
8 in.

1._____

2._____

3._____

4._____

5._____

6._____

7._____

8._____

Find the missing dimension of the solid. Round your answer to the nearest tenth.

5. Volume = 502 ft^3
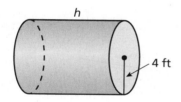
h
4 ft

6. Volume = 85 yd^3
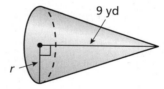
9 yd
r

7. A cylindrical tank can hold 2279.64 cubic feet of water. The radius of the tank is 11 feet. What is the height of the tank?

8. Double both dimensions of the cylinder. How many times greater is the volume of the new cylinder than the volume of the original cylinder?
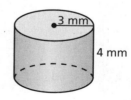
3 mm
4 mm

Chapter 8 **Quiz**
For use after Section 8.4

Find the volume of the sphere. Round your answer to the nearest tenth.

Answers

1.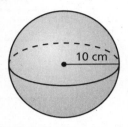
   10 cm

2.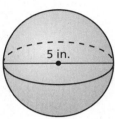
   5 in.

1. _____

2. _____

3. _____

4. _____

5. _____

6. _____

7. _____

8. _____

9. _____

10. _____

Find the radius of the sphere with the given volume.

3. Volume $= 36\pi$ in.^{3}

4. Volume $= \dfrac{9}{16}\pi$ ft^3

5. Find the volume of the composite solid. Round your answer to the nearest tenth.

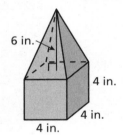
6 in.
4 in.
4 in.
4 in.

6. Determine whether the solids are similar.

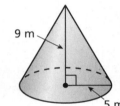
8 m   9 m
4 m   5 m

The solids are similar. Find the missing dimension or surface area.

7.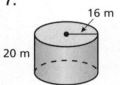
16 m
20 m   25 m b

8.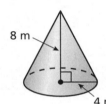
14 ft
Surface Area = 1240 ft^2

7 ft
Surface Area = ?

9. Find the volume of the inflatable crayon.

|—12 in.—|
8 in.
Crayon
|——— 40 in. ———|

10. The ratio of the corresponding linear measures of two similar triangular prisms is 2 to 5. The larger triangular prism has a volume of 150 cubic centimeters. Find the volume of the smaller triangular prism.

Name_____ Date _____

Chapter 8 Test A

Find the volume of the solid. Round your answer to the nearest tenth.

Answers

1.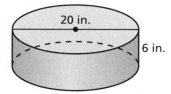

20 in.

6 in.

2.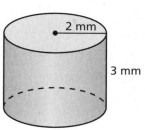

2 mm

3 mm

3.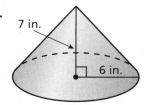

7 in.

6 in.

4.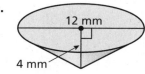

12 mm

4 mm

5.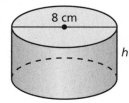

4.2 ft

6.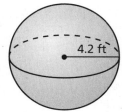

6.8 ft

1. _____

2. _____

3. _____

4. _____

5. _____

6. _____

7. _____

8. _____

9. _____

10. _____

Find the missing dimension of the solid. Round your answer to the nearest tenth.

7.

8 cm

h

Volume = 201 cm³

8.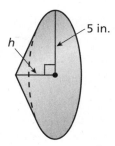

5 in.

h

Volume = 79 in.³

Find the radius of the sphere with the given volume.

9. Volume = $\dfrac{1}{6}\pi$ ft³

10. Volume = $\dfrac{32}{3}\pi$ yd³

Chapter 8 **Test A** (continued)

Find the volume of the composite solid.

Answers

11.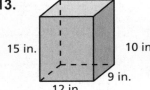

5 cm

4 cm

10 cm

4 cm

12.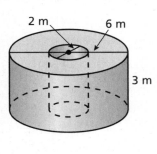

2 m   6 m

3 m

11. _____

12. _____

13. _____

14. _____

15. _____

16. _____

17. _____

18. _____

Determine whether the solids are similar.

13.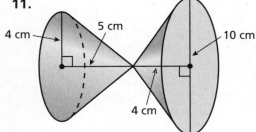

15 in.

12 in.

9 in.

10 in.

8 in.

6 in.

14.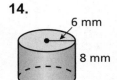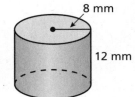

6 mm

8 mm

8 mm

12 mm

The solids are similar. Find the surface area *S* or the volume *V* of the larger solid.

19. _____

20. _____

15.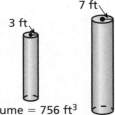

3 ft

7 ft

Volume = 756 ft³

16.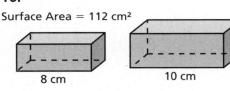

Surface Area = 112 cm²

8 cm

10 cm

17. A water cooler is in the shape of a cylinder with a diameter of 2 feet and a height of 3 feet. About how many gallons of water can the cooler contain? Round your answer to the nearest whole number.

$\left(1 \text{ ft}^3 \approx 7.5 \text{ gal}\right)$

18. The volume of a cone is 6π cubic inches. What is the volume of a cylinder having the same base and same height? Explain your reasoning.

19. A similar scale model of the motorcycle shown stands 3 inches high and is 6 inches long. How high does the actual motorcycle stand?

├── 96 in. ──┤

20. A hatchling turtle has a shell with a 1-inch diameter. The shell keeps a similar shape as the turtle grows. Compare the volume and surface area of the hatchling's shell to the shell when its diameter is 4 inches.

Name_____ Date_____

Find the volume of the solid. Round your answer to the nearest tenth.

Answers

1.

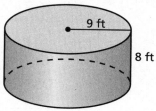

9 ft
8 ft

2.

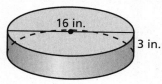

16 in.
3 in.

1. _____

2. _____

3. _____

4. _____

5. _____

6. _____

7. _____

8. _____

9. _____

10. _____

11. _____

_____

3.

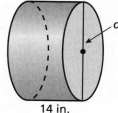

10 mm
22 mm

4.

4.8 ft
6 ft

5.

25 cm

6.

34 mm

Find the missing dimension of the solid. Round your answer to the nearest tenth.

7.

d

14 in.

Volume = 7433 in.^{3}

8.

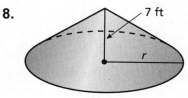

7 ft
r

Volume = 733 ft^3

Find the radius of the sphere with the given volume.

9. Volume = $\dfrac{9}{250}\pi$ m^3

10. Volume = 4500π mm^3

11. What happens to the volume of a rectangular prism when the length and width are doubled and the height is tripled?

Chapter 8 **Test B** (continued)

Find the volume of the composite solid. Round your answer to the nearest tenth.

12.

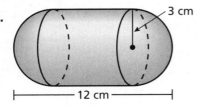

3 cm

├───── 12 cm ─────┤

13.

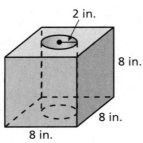

2 in.

8 in.

8 in.

8 in.

12. _____

13. _____

14. _____

15. _____

16. _____

17. _____

18. _____

19. _____

_____

_____

_____

_____

_____

20. a._____

b._____

Determine whether the solids are similar.

14.

16 in.

10 in.

12 in.   6 in.

14 in.   8 in.

15.

15 m

9 m

12 m

20 m   15 m

25 m

The solids are similar. Find the surface area S or the volume V of the smaller solid.

16. Volume = 3160 ft³

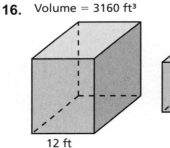

8 ft

12 ft

17.

15 mm   12 mm

Surface Area = 560 mm²

18. A juice can is in the shape of a cylinder with a diameter of 4 inches. It has a volume of 125 cubic inches. What is the height of the can? Round your answer to the nearest whole number.

19. Compare the amount of sand in the top cone of the hourglass to the amount there will be when the height of the sand in the top cone is only 1 inch. Explain.

10 in.

20. You buy a cylindrical container of salt with a diameter of 3.25 inches and a height of 5 inches. Your salt shaker is a cylinder with a diameter of 1 inch and a height of 1.5 inches.

   a. Are the cylinders similar?

   b. How many times can you fill your salt shaker with the container? Round your answer to the nearest tenth.

Chapter 8 Standards Assessment

1. List the ordered pairs shown in the mapping diagram.

Input   Output

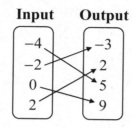

A. $(-4, 5), (-2, -3), (0, 9), (2, 2)$ C. $(-4, 9), (-2, 5), (0, 2), (2, -3)$

B. $(-4, -3), (-2, 2), (0, 5), (2, 9)$ D. $(-3, -2), (2, 2), (5, -4), (9, 0)$

2. **GRIDDED RESPONSE** Evaluate the following expression.

$$\sqrt[3]{64}$$

3. Solve the equation below for x.

$$2(x + 5) = 3(x - 4)$$

F. $-\dfrac{22}{5}$ H. $\dfrac{22}{5}$

G. -2 I. 22

4. What is the approximate volume of the perfume in the perfume bottle?

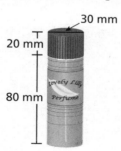

A. 8954 cubic millimeters   C. 56,549 cubic millimeters

B. 10,838 cubic millimeters   D. 70,686 cubic millimeters

Chapter 8 **Standards Assessment** (continued)

5. What value of *n* makes the equation below true?

$$\frac{n}{2} - 6 = -14$$

   F. −40   **H.** −10

   G. −16   **I.** −4

6. Which equation represents a line with a slope of −3 that goes through the point $(2, 1)$?

   A. $y = 3x + 7$ **C.** $y = -3x + 7$

   B. $y = -3x + 1$ **D.** $y = 3x + 1$

7. A right circular cone and its dimensions are shown below. What is the approximate volume of the cone?

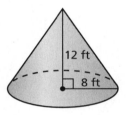

   F. 100.53 cubic feet   **H.** 804.24 cubic feet

   G. 502.40 cubic feet   **I.** 2412.74 cubic feet

8. SHORT RESPONSE The figure below is a diagram for making a tin lantern.

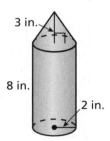

What is the approximate volume, in cubic inches, of the entire lantern? Show your work and explain your reasoning.

1. **A.** Correct answer
   B. The student ignores the arrows and pairs the inputs with the outputs that are horizontal from the input.
   C. The student ignores the arrows and pairs the inputs with incorrect outputs.
   D. The student switches the inputs and the outputs in the ordered pairs.

2. Correct answer: 4

   Common error: The student takes the square root of 64 resulting in an answer of 8.

3. **F.** The student adds the coefficients of x and makes a sign error.
   G. The student subtracts 12 from each side instead of adding 12.
   H. The student adds the coefficients of x.
   I. Correct answer

4. **A.** The student finds the surface area of the part containing the perfume.
   B. The student finds the surface area of the entire bottle.
   C. Correct answer
   D. The student includes the lid when finding the volume.

5. **F.** The student adds -6 to both sides and then multiplies both sides by 2.
   G. Correct answer
   H. The student adds -6 to both sides and then divides -20 by 2.
   I. The student adds 6 to both sides and then divides -8 by 2.

6. **A.** The student forgets to include the negative sign for the slope in the equation.
   B. The student thinks the y-intercept is the y-coordinate of the given point.
   C. Correct answer
   D. The student forgets to include the negative sign for the slope in the equation and thinks the y-intercept is the y-coordinate of the given point.

7. **F.** The student forgets to square the radius.
   G. The student uses the formula for the surface area of a cone.
   H. Correct answer
   I. The student forgets to multiply by $\frac{1}{3}$.

8. **2 points** The student demonstrates a thorough understanding of finding the volume of a cylinder and a cone. The student correctly finds a volume of 113.1 cubic inches. The student provides clear and complete work and explanations.

1 point The student demonstrates a partial understanding of finding the volume of a cylinder and a cone. The student provides some correct work and explanation toward finding the volumes.

0 points The student demonstrates insufficient understanding of finding the volume of a cylinder and a cone. The student does not make any meaningful progress toward finding the volumes.

Chapter 8 Alternative Assessment

1. Sarah made two cylinders.

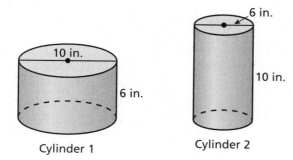

Cylinder 1

Cylinder 2

a. Predict which cylinder has the greater volume.

b. Find the volume of each cylinder. Round your answer to the nearest tenth. Was your prediction in part (a) correct? Explain.

2. Sarah also made two cones.

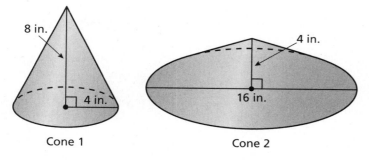

Cone 1

Cone 2

a. Predict which cone has the greater volume.

b. Find the volume of each cone. Round your answer to the nearest tenth. Was your prediction in part (a) correct? Explain.

Chapter 8 Alternative Assessment Rubric

Score	Conceptual Understanding	Mathematical Skills	Work Habits
4	Shows complete understanding of: • visualizing 3-dimensional shapes • the concept and formulas for finding the volume of cylinders and cones	Makes accurate predictions. Correctly calculates the volume of all solids.	Answers all parts of both problems. All calculations are done in a systematic way. Work is very neat and well organized.
3	Shows nearly complete understanding of: • visualizing 3-dimensional shapes • the concept and formulas for finding the volume of cylinders and cones	Makes some accurate predictions. Correctly calculates the volume of most solids.	Answers most parts of both problems. Most calculations are done in a systematic way. Work is somewhat neat and organized.
2	Shows some understanding of: • visualizing 3-dimensional shapes • the concept and formulas for finding the volume of cylinders and cones	Makes one accurate predictions. Correctly calculates the volume of a few solids.	Answers some parts of both problems. Some calculations are done in a systematic way. Work is not neat or organized.
1	Shows little understanding of: • visualizing 3-dimensional shapes • the concept and formulas for finding the volume of cylinders and cones	Makes no accurate predictions. Incorrectly calculates the volume of the solids.	Does not answer all parts of both problems. No calculations are done in a systematic way. Work is sloppy and disorganized.

Name_____ Date_____

1. The scatter plot shows the number
   of male teachers in a school district
   from 2006 to 2012.

   a. In what school year did the school
   district have 41 male teachers?

   b. How many male teachers did the
   district have in the 2012 school year?

   c. Describe the relationship shown
   by the data.

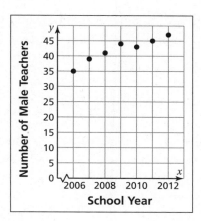

Answers

1. a._____

   b._____

   c._____

2. _____

   _____

   _____

3. _____

Describe the relationship between the data. Identify any outliers, gaps, or clusters.

2.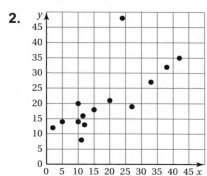

3.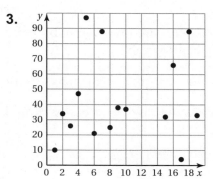

   _____

   _____

4. a.___See left.___

   b._____

   c._____

4. The table shows the number of members at a gym each month from
   January to July.

Month	1	2	3	4	5	6	7
Members	20	34	40	45	50	52	60

   _____

   _____

   d._____

   a. Make a scatter plot of the data
   and draw a line of fit.

   b. Write an equation of the line
   of fit.

   c. Interpret the slope and the
   y-intercept of the line of fit.

   d. Predict how many members
   the gym will have in December.

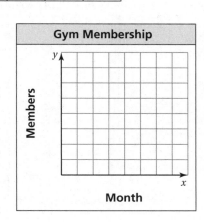

Name _____ Date _____

Chapter 9 **Quiz**
For use after Section 9.4

1. You randomly survey students about their involvement in school sports and the school music program. The two-way table shows the results.

		Sports		
		Involved	Not Involved	Total
Music Program	Involved	62	34	
	Not Involved	41	27	
	Total			

Answers

1. a._____

 b._____

 c.___See left.___

 _____

 _____

2. _____

 _____

3. _____

 _____

4. _____

 _____

5. _____

 _____

6. _____

 _____

7. _____

 _____

 _____

 _____

   a. How many students are involved in the school music program but not school sports?

   b. What percent of students are involved in both school sports and the school music program?

   c. Find and interpret the marginal frequencies for the survey.

Choose an appropriate data display for the situation. Explain your reasoning.

2. the profits of a company over a year

3. a person's income based on age

4. percent of student athletes in each sport

5. the numbers and types of different species of fish at an aquarium

Explain why the data display is misleading.

6.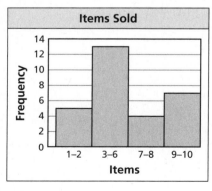

7.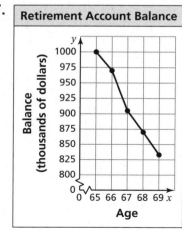

Chapter 9 Test A

1. The scatter plot shows the total earnings (fare and tips) of a taxi driver during one day.

   a. How many rides did the taxi driver give to earn $175?

   b. About how much did the taxi driver earn for giving 2 rides?

   c. Describe the relationship shown by the data.

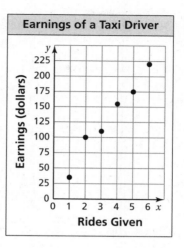

Earnings of a Taxi Driver

Rides Given

Answers

1. a._____

   b._____

   c._____

2. a.___See left.___

   b._____

   c._____

   _____

   _____

   d._____

3. _____

   _____

   _____

   _____

4. _____

   _____

   _____

2. The table shows the total inches of rain that had fallen after each hour.

Hour	0	1	2	3	4	5
Inches of Rain	0	0.5	1.1	1.8	2.4	3.0

   a. Make a scatter plot of the data and draw a line of fit.

   b. Write an equation of the line of fit.

   c. Interpret the slope and y-intercept of the line of fit.

   d. If it continues to rain at a similar rate, predict how much rain will have fallen after 8 hours.

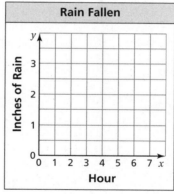

Rain Fallen

Hour

Describe the relationship between the data. Identify any outliers, gaps, or clusters.

3.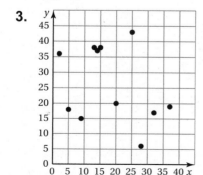

4.

Chapter 9 **Test A** (continued)

Choose an appropriate data display for the situation. Explain your reasoning.

5. the daily high temperature in your town

6. the ages of people at a play

7. the percents of a company's revenue that come from different sources

Explain why the data display is misleading.

8. **Favorite Class**

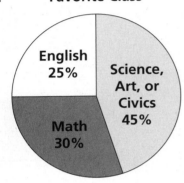

9.
Instruments Played

Guitar

Saxophone

Piano

🎸 = 1 guitar   🎷 = 1 saxophone
🎹 = 1 piano

10. You randomly survey students about whether they ate or skipped lunch and breakfast. The results of the survey are shown in the two-way table.

a. How many students in the survey skipped breakfast but ate lunch?

		Breakfast		
		Ate	Skipped	Total
Lunch	Ate	40	12	
	Skipped	8	0	
	Total			

b. How many of the students in the survey ate lunch?

c. How many students were surveyed?

d. Find and interpret the marginal frequencies for the survey.

e. What percent of students skipped breakfast but ate lunch?

Chapter 9 Test B

1. The scatter plot shows the numbers of hybrid vehicles sold in a city from 2009 to 2014.

   a. In what year were 400 hybrid vehicles sold?

   b. About how many hybrid vehicles were sold in 2012?

   c. Describe the relationship shown by the data.

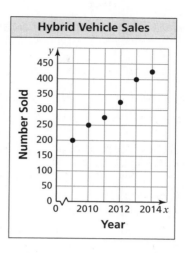

Hybrid Vehicle Sales

Answers

1. a._____

   b._____

   c._____

2. a.___See left.___

   b._____

   c._____

   _____

   _____

   d._____

3. _____

   _____

   _____

4. _____

   _____

   _____

2. The table shows the number of birds observed at a feeder each week.

Week	1	2	3	4	5	6
Birds	46	40	39	35	30	27

   a. Make a scatter plot of the data and draw a line of fit.

   b. Write an equation of the line of fit.

   c. Interpret the slope and *y*-intercept of the line of fit.

   d. Estimate how many birds were at the feeder 3 weeks before week 1.

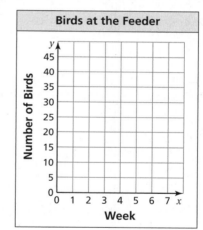

Birds at the Feeder

Describe the relationship between the data. Identify any outliers, gaps, or clusters.

3.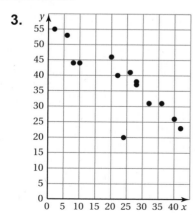

4.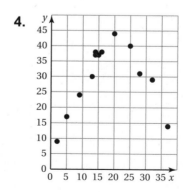

Name _____ Date _____

Choose an appropriate data display for the situation. Explain your reasoning.

Answers

5. number of wins for each team in a baseball league at the end of the season

6. the prices of a flat screen television set at twenty different stores

Explain why the data display is misleading.

7.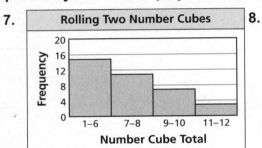

8.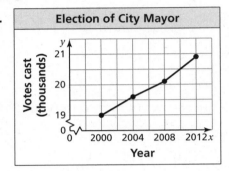

5. _____

   _____

   _____

6. _____

   _____

   _____

7. _____

8. _____

9. a. __See left.__

   b. _____

9. You randomly survey students in your class about whether they visited an amusement park in the summer. The results are shown.

Visited an Amusement Park
Boys: 38
Girls: 29

Did Not Visit an Amusement Park
Boys: 17
Girls: 25

   c. _____

   a. Make a two-way table that includes the marginal frequencies.

		Visited an Amusement Park		
		Yes	No	Total
Student	Boys			
	Girls			
	Total			

   b. Interpret the marginal frequencies for the survey.

   c. For each gender, what percent of the students visited an amusement park?

Chapter 9 **Standards Assessment**

1. The owner of an arcade measured the outside temperature each Saturday at noon and recorded the number of people in the arcade. The scatter plot shows the data collected. Which description fits the data in the scatter plot?

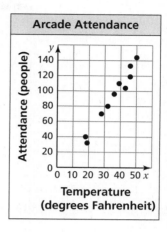

Arcade Attendance

A. As temperature increases, more people come to the arcade.

B. As temperature increases, fewer people come to the arcade.

C. The number of people at the arcade is always the same.

D. There is no relationship between temperature and the number of people at the arcade.

2. **GRIDDED RESPONSE** Find the value of x.

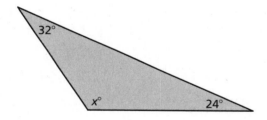

3. Find the distance between the points in the coordinate grid below.

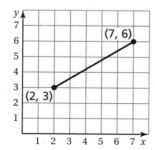

F. $\sqrt{8}$ **H.** $\sqrt{34}$

G. 4   **I.** 8

Chapter 9 **Standards Assessment** (continued)

4. Use the table below. Which linear function relates *y* to *x*?

x	1	3	5	7	9
y	11	9	7	5	3

   A. $y = 11x$ **C.** $y = -x + 12$

   B. $y = -2x + 13$ **D.** $y = x - 2$

5. The graph shows the cost of attending the school fair. What is the slope of the line?

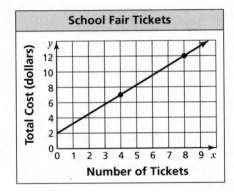

   F. 0.8   **H.** 1.25

   G. 1   **I.** 2

6. What value of *x* makes the equation below true?

$$4x + 8 = 18 + 2x$$

   A. 2.5   **C.** 6.5

   B. 5   **D.** 13

7. **EXTENDED RESPONSE** The table shows the annual expenses of a company.

Category	Salary	Rent	Insurance	Utilities	Other
Annual Expenses (thousands of dollars)	450	84	36	24	50

   Part A   You are asked how this data could be displayed effectively. Make **two** suggestions, and explain why you think each is a good choice.

   Part B   Give **two** data displays that would ineffectively display the data. Explain why you think each is not a good choice.

1. **A.** Correct answer
   B. The student misreads the nature of the graph, overlooking the positive relationship shown by the data. The student reads the graph from right to left.
   C. The student misreads the nature of the graph, overlooking the positive relationship shown by the data.
   D. The student focuses on the points that model a slight decrease in attendance.

2. Correct answer: 124

   Common error: The student assumes there are 100 degrees in a triangle, yielding an answer of 44.

3. **F.** The student finds the square root of the sum of the positive differences between coordinates.
   G. The student finds $\sqrt{8}$ as in choice F but thinks that the root is 4.
   H. Correct answer
   I. The student finds the sum of the positive differences between coordinates.

4. **A.** The student picks the simplest linear function that fits the first point in the table.
   B. The student incorrectly calculates the slope, writes an equation, and tests only the first point.
   C. Correct answer
   D. The student analyzes the relationship among the y-values and selects an equation that most closely expresses that relationship.

5. **F.** The student reverses the roles of x and y in the slope formula.
   G. The student miscounts squares when calculating slope.
   H. Correct answer
   I. The student picks the y-intercept instead of the slope.

6. **A.** The student calculates $18 - 8$ correctly, but then miscalculates $4x - 2x$, ignoring the coefficient of $2x$.
   B. Correct answer
   C. The student adds 8 and 18 instead of subtracting, and then miscalculates $4x - 2x$, ignoring the coefficient of $2x$.
   D. The student adds 8 and 18 instead of subtracting.

7. **4 points** The student demonstrates a thorough understanding of choosing efficient and inefficient ways to display data.

    3 points The student demonstrates an essential but less than thorough understanding of choosing efficient and inefficient ways to display data.

    2 points The student's explanations demonstrate a lack of essential understanding for choosing efficient and inefficient ways to display data.

    1 point The student demonstrates limited understanding. The student's response is incomplete and exhibits many flaws.

    0 points The student provides no response, a completely incorrect or incomprehensible response, or a response that demonstrates insufficient understanding of choosing efficient and inefficient ways to display data.

Chapter 9 Alternative Assessment

1. You play a game with the spinner shown. The table shows the number of times you spin a 6 during the game.

Number of Spins	0	25	50	75	100	125	150	175	200
Number of Times You Spin a 6	0	5	10	12	16	22	26	29	35

    a. Describe the relationship shown by the data.

    b. Make a scatter plot of the data.

    c. Draw a line of fit.

    d. Write an equation of the line of fit.

    e. How many times do you think you will spin a 6 if you spin the spinner 300 times?

Chapter 9 **Alternative Assessment Rubric**

Score	Conceptual Understanding	Mathematical Skills	Work Habits
4	Shows complete understanding of: • scatter plots • lines of fit • making predictions	Graphs the scatter plot and the line of fit accurately. Accurately calculates all predictions.	Answers all parts of the question. All answers and the graph are written in a systematic way. Work is very neat and well organized.
3	Shows nearly complete understanding of: • scatter plots • lines of fit • making predictions	Graphs the scatter plot and the line of fit accurately. Accurately calculates most predictions.	Answers almost all parts of the question. Most answers and the graph are written in a systematic way. Work is neat and organized.
2	Shows some understanding of: • scatter plots • lines of fit • making predictions	Graphs the scatter plot accurately but not the line of fit. Accurately calculates some predictions.	Answers some parts of the question. Some answers and the graph are written in a systematic way. Work is not very neat or organized.
1	Shows little understanding of: • scatter plots • lines of fit • making predictions	Does not graph the scatter plot or the line of fit accurately. Does not make accurate predictions.	Does not attempt any part of the question. No answers nor the graph are written. Work is sloppy and disorganized.

Name_____ Date_____

Chapter 10 Quiz
For use after Section 10.4

Write the product using exponents.

1. $\dfrac{1}{5} \cdot \dfrac{1}{5} \cdot \dfrac{1}{5} \cdot \dfrac{1}{5} \cdot \dfrac{1}{5}$ **2.** $(-2) \cdot (-2) \cdot (-2)$

3. $y \cdot y \cdot y \cdot y \cdot y \cdot y$ **4.** $4 \cdot 4 \cdot 4 \cdot c \cdot c$

Evaluate the expression.

5. 2^4 **6.** $(-3)^3$

7. $\dfrac{3^4}{3^5}$ **8.** $(-2.6)^4 (-2.6)^{-4}$

Simplify the expression. Write your answer as a power.

9. $(-1)^3 \cdot (-1)^2$ **10.** $\left(b^4\right)^2$

Simplify the expression.

11. $(4f)^3$ **12.** $\left(-\dfrac{3}{8}t^2\right)^2$

Simplify the expression. Write your answer as a power.

13. $\dfrac{(-2)^{10}}{(-2)^5}$ **14.** $\dfrac{5^4 \cdot 5^9}{5^6}$

15. $\dfrac{x^{14}}{x^4 \cdot x^2}$ **16.** $\dfrac{y^3}{y^{11}} \cdot \dfrac{y^{21}}{y^9}$

Simplify. Write the expression using only positive exponents.

17. $4c^{-5}c^2$ **18.** $\dfrac{3x^2}{9x^5}$

19. Is $x^3 x^5$ equivalent to x^{15}? Explain. If not, what expression is equivalent to $x^3 x^5$?

20. Find the value of x that makes $\dfrac{(-2)^{4x+2}}{(-2)^{2x}} = (-2)^{12}$ true.

Answers

1. _____
2. _____
3. _____
4. _____
5. _____
6. _____
7. _____
8. _____
9. _____
10. _____
11. _____
12. _____
13. _____
14. _____
15. _____
16. _____
17. _____
18. _____
19. _____
    _____
    _____
20. _____

Chapter 10 **Quiz**
For use after Section 10.7

Tell whether the number is written in scientific notation. Explain.

1. 0.3×10^4

2. 12×10^{-7}

Write the number in standard form.

3. -2.7×10^{-2}

4. 4×10^6

Write the number in scientific notation.

5. 0.0031

6. $741,000$

Order the numbers from least to greatest.

7. $3.9 \times 10^7,\ 3.08 \times 10^7,\ 3.88 \times 10^7$

8. $6.5 \times 10^{-4},\ 5.2 \times 10^{-3},\ 8.1 \times 10^{-5}$

Evaluate the expression. Write your answer in scientific notation.

9. $\left(4.1 \times 10^3\right) + \left(3.7 \times 10^2\right)$

10. $\left(9.3 \times 10^{-3}\right) - \left(6.9 \times 10^{-4}\right)$

11. $\left(1.2 \times 10^{-3}\right) \times \left(4 \times 10^5\right)$

12. $\left(8 \times 10^{-6}\right) \div 1.6$

13. One meter is 1.0×10^9 nanometers. How many square nanometers are in 2 square meters?

14. You fill a large water tank with 3.4×10^3 gallons of water. About 6.1% of the water is not fresh water. How many gallons of fresh water are in the tank?

15. The distance between two cities is 4000 kilometers.

 a. One kilometer is 10^6 millimeters. What is the distance between the two cities in millimeters?

 b. Two other cities are 4×10^8 millimeters away from each other. Are these two cities closer or farther away from each other than the other two cities? Explain.

Answers

1. _____

   _____

2. _____

   _____

3. _____

4. _____

5. _____

6. _____

7. _____

   _____

8. _____

   _____

9. _____

10. _____

11. _____

12. _____

13. _____

14. _____

15. a. _____

   b. _____

   _____

   _____

   _____

Chapter 10 **Test A**

Evaluate the expression.

Answers

1. $\left(\dfrac{1}{3}\right)^3$

2. 2^5

3. $(-3)^4$

4. $\dfrac{1}{3}\left(2^4 + 2\right)$

5. $9^2 - 4^3$

6. $\dfrac{3}{4^2} + \dfrac{5}{2^3}$

7. A new television program attracts 1.1 times as many viewers each week as the week before.

    a. If 2 million people watch the premiere, how many watch the week after that?

    b. Write and evaluate an expression to find the number of viewers 4 weeks after the premiere. Round to the nearest tenth of a million.

8. The distance traveled by a falling rock is modeled by $d = 5t^2$, where d is the distance in meters and t is the time in seconds.

    a. Write and simplify an expression for the distance the rock falls in $2t$ seconds. Is it twice as far? Explain your reasoning.

    b. The rock falls 15 meters in t seconds. How far does it fall in $2t$ seconds?

Simplify the expression.

9. $(3x)^4$

10. $\dfrac{2^5}{2^4}$

11. $\dfrac{(4a)^3}{a^5}$

12. $\dfrac{3^3 x^2}{3x}$

13. $\left(4x^2\right)(2xy)^3$

14. $w^3\left(w^2 \bullet w^5\right)$

15. A pollen grain is $\dfrac{3}{10^3}$ centimeters wide. In an illustration, the pollen grain is 6 centimeters wide. How much larger is the illustration than the actual pollen?

Answers

1. _____

2. _____

3. _____

4. _____

5. _____

6. _____

7. a._____

   b._____

   _____

8. a.___See left.___

   b._____

9. _____

10. _____

11. _____

12. _____

13. _____

14. _____

15. _____

Chapter 10 **Test A** (continued)

16. There is 10^{-3} gram in a milligram, and there are 10^6 grams in a metric ton. How many metric tons are there in a milligram?

Simplify. Write the expression using only positive exponents.

17. $8w^{-5}$

18. $2x^{-3} \cdot 5x^{-7}$

19. $\dfrac{(2g)^{-3}}{(fg)^2}$

Write the number in standard form.

20. 5×10^4

21. 7.9×10^{-4}

22. 6.999×10^{10}

Evaluate the expression. Write your answer in scientific notation.

23. $\left(7.5 \times 10^{-3}\right) + \left(5.8 \times 10^{-3}\right)$

24. $\left(4.6 \times 10^6\right) - \left(8.3 \times 10^5\right)$

25. $\left(1.1 \times 10^8\right) \times \left(1.4 \times 10^7\right)$

26. $\left(1.6 \times 10^{-4}\right) \div \left(8 \times 10^3\right)$

27. A blue star has a temperature between 36,000°F and 90,000°F.

   a. Write the temperature range using scientific notation.

   b. Is a star with temperature 8.8×10^3 degrees Fahrenheit *warmer* or *cooler* than a blue star?

28. The diameter of a white dwarf is 1.0×10^{-1} times the diameter of our Sun. The Sun is 1.4×10^6 kilometers wide. How wide is the white dwarf?

29. Mercury is 3.6×10^6 miles from the Sun. Pluto is 3.6×10^9 miles from the Sun. How many times farther from the Sun is Pluto than Mercury?

30. A gymnasium is 100 yards wide, 150 yards long, and 30 yards tall.

   a. Write the dimensions in scientific notation.

   b. Find the volume of the building. Write your answer in scientific notation.

   c. The cooling system is designed to cool a building up to 5.0×10^5 cubic yards. What size addition could be added to the gym without needing a new cooling system?

Answers

16. _____

17. _____

18. _____

19. _____

20. _____

21. _____

22. _____

23. _____

24. _____

25. _____

26. _____

27. a. __See left.__

    b._____

28. _____

29. _____

30. a. __See left.__

    b._____

    c._____

Name_____ Date _____

Evaluate the expression.

Answers

1. 7^2

2. $(-3)^5$

3. $1 - \left(\dfrac{1}{5}\right)^3$

4. $\dfrac{1}{6^2} + \dfrac{5}{6}$

5. $8^3 - 8^2$

6. $-\left(\dfrac{1}{4}\right)^3$

7. You run $\dfrac{1}{2}$ mile on Sunday. On each day after the weekend, you run 1.5 times as far as you did the day before.

    a. How far do you run Monday?

    b. Write and evaluate an expression to find the distance you run 5 days after Sunday (Friday). Round to the nearest tenth of a mile.

8. The kinetic energy in joules of a 50-kilogram runner running at v meters per second is modeled by the equation $E = 25v^2$.

    a. Write and simplify an expression for the kinetic energy of a runner running at $3v$ meters per second. Is it three times as great as the kinetic energy at v meters per second? Explain your reasoning.

    b. The kinetic energy of a runner running at v meters per second is 70 joules. What is the runner's kinetic energy at $3v$ meters per second?

Simplify the expression.

9. $\left(\dfrac{3}{4}w\right)^2$

10. $\dfrac{3^5}{3^2}$

11. $\dfrac{b^6}{(2b)^3}$

12. $\dfrac{5^7 a}{5^4 a^2}$

13. $\left(3^2 x^4\right)(-2x)^3$

14. $\dfrac{q^2 \cdot q^5}{q^7}$

15. The distance between two towns is 80 kilometers, or 8×10^6 centimeters. On a map the distance is 40 centimeters. How much larger is the actual distance than the map distance?

Answers

1. _____
2. _____
3. _____
4. _____
5. _____
6. _____
7. a._____
   b._____
   _____
8. a.___See left.___
   b._____
9. _____
10. _____
11. _____
12. _____
13. _____
14. _____
15. _____

Chapter 10 **Test B** (continued)

16. There is 10^{-2} meter in a centimeter. How many square meters are there in a square centimeter?

Answers

Simplify. Write the expression using only positive exponents.

17. $\dfrac{2z^{-3}}{4z^{-5}}$ **18.** $12x^{-7} \cdot 5x^{-4}$ **19.** $\dfrac{(ab)^{-3}}{a^2}$

Write the number in standard form.

20. 7.05×10^6 **21.** 2.0×10^{-1} **22.** 4.773×10^8

Evaluate the expression. Write your answer in scientific notation.

23. $\left(3.1 \times 10^7\right) + \left(5.5 \times 10^5\right)$ **24.** $\left(6.8 \times 10^{-3}\right) - \left(8.5 \times 10^{-4}\right)$

25. $\left(8.3 \times 10^3\right) \times \left(3 \times 10^{-6}\right)$ **26.** $\left(6 \times 10^{-4}\right) \div \left(1.5 \times 10^{-6}\right)$

27. At Mercury's closest approach to the Sun it is 46,000,000 kilometers away. At its farthest distance it is 69,800,000 kilometers away.

     a. Write the distance range using scientific notation.

     b. Is Mercury ever 5.8×10^7 kilometers from the Sun?

28. The image of a dust mite from a scanning electron microscope is 1.5×10^2 millimeters wide. The image is 5×10^2 times life size. How many millimeters wide is the dust mite?

29. The eye of a needle is 0.1 centimeter wide, 0.3 centimeter tall, and 0.05 centimeter deep.

     a. Write the dimensions in scientific notation.

     b. Find the volume of the eye of the needle, assuming it is rectangular. Write your answer in scientific notation.

     c. An artist installs minuscule bits of glass, each of which has a volume of 0.00003 cubic centimeter. How many pieces could fit in the eye of the needle?

Answers

16. _____

17. _____

18. _____

19. _____

20. _____

21. _____

22. _____

23. _____

24. _____

25. _____

26. _____

27. a. _**See left.**_

     b._____

28. _____

29. a. _**See left.**_

     b._____

     c._____

Chapter 10 Standards Assessment

1. The steps Antonio took to write 4.0×10^{-3} in standard form are given below. What should Antonio change in order to write the number correctly?

$$4.1 \times 10^{-3} = 4.100$$
$$= 4100$$

A. Keep 4.1 and attach three zeroes at the end.

B. Move the decimal point one place to the right and attach three zeroes at the end of 41.

C. Multiply 10 times -3 and then multiply the product by 4.1.

D. Move the decimal point three places to the left.

2. GRIDDED RESPONSE Find the value of x.

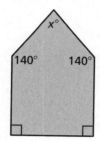

3. The mass of a grain of sand is about 10^{-3} gram. About how many grains of sand are there in a 2-kilogram bag of sand?

F. 1,000

H. 200,000

G. 2,000

I. 2,000,000

4. A baseball diamond is a square with a side length of 90 feet. Third base and first base form opposite corners of the square. When a fielder throws the ball from third base to a fielder at first base, how far is the throw?

A. 90 feet

C. about 135 feet

B. about 127 feet

D. 180 feet

Chapter 10 **Standards Assessment** (continued)

5. The body length of a daddy long-legs spider is about 0.000002 kilometer. Write this length in scientific notation.

    F. 2.0×10^{-6} kilometer   **H.** 2.0×10^{5} kilometer

    G. 2.0×10^{-5} kilometer   **I.** 2.0×10^{6} kilometer

6. What is the slope of the line shown in the graph below?

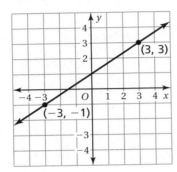

    A. $-\dfrac{2}{3}$ **C.** 1

    B. $\dfrac{2}{3}$ **D.** $\dfrac{3}{2}$

7. Which transformation is shown below?

    F. translation   **H.** rotation

    G. reflection   **I.** dilation

8. SHORT RESPONSE Two students disagree over the meaning of the expression $9^6 \bullet 9^7$. One student says that it equals 9^{13}. The other student says that it equals 9^{42}. The first student says that the rule is to add exponents. The second student says that the rule is to multiply exponents. Show the students step-by-step why one of the rules is correct.

Standards Assessment Item Analysis

1. **A.** The student has forgotten to move the decimal point before adding zeros.

   B. The student has moved the decimal point in the wrong direction and 4 places instead of 3.

   C. The student has misunderstood that 10^{-3} acts as a base raised to an exponent.

   D. Correct answer

2. Correct answer: 80

   Common error: The student thinks it should be a right angle, and writes 90 as an answer.

3. **F.** The student finds 10^3.

   G. The student finds 10^3 and multiplies by 2 because it is a 2-kilogram bag.

   H. The student incorrectly converts kilograms to grams, multiplying by 100 instead of 1,000.

   I. Correct answer

4. **A.** The student thinks the three sides of the triangle are equal.

   B. Correct answer

   C. The student does not use the Pythagorean Theorem, and either estimates the distance or adds half of 90 to 90.

   D. The student adds the lengths of the two sides to get the third side.

5. **F.** Correct answer

   G. The student miscounts the number of decimal places.

   H. The student miscounts the number of decimal places and forgets the negative in the exponent.

   I. The student forgets the negative in the exponent.

6. **A.** The student makes a sign error in finding the slope.

   B. Correct answer

   C. The student thinks that the y-intercept is the slope.

   D. The student finds the inverse of the slope.

7. **F.** The student mistakes the rotation for a translation.

   G. The student mistakes the rotation for a reflection.

   H. Correct answer

   I. The student mistakes the rotation for a dilation.

8. **2 points** The student demonstrates a thorough understanding of the product of powers property, applies it accurately, and writes out multiplication factors clearly to show why $9^6 \cdot 9^7 = 9^{13}$.

   1 point The student demonstrates a partial understanding of the product of powers property. The result $9^6 \cdot 9^7 = 9^{13}$ is stated correctly but the attempt to validate the conclusion is weak, at best.

   0 points The student provides no response, a completely incorrect or incomprehensible response, or a response that demonstrates insufficient understanding of the product of powers property.

Chapter 10 **Alternative Assessment**

1. Martha wanted to investigate an idea about exponents, so she wrote the following expressions.

$$x^2y^{-3} \qquad x^{-2}y^3 \qquad x^2y^3 \qquad x^{-2}y^{-3} \qquad \frac{x^2}{y^{-3}} \qquad \frac{x^{-2}}{y^3} \qquad \frac{x^2}{y^3} \qquad \frac{x^{-2}}{y^{-3}}$$

   a. Evaluate each expression for $x = 3$ and $y = 2$.

   b. What relationships do you notice among the evaluated expressions in part (a)?

   c. Choose two other values for x and y and evaluate the expressions again.

   d. What relationships do you notice among the evaluated expressions in part (c)?

   e. Explain why the original expressions that Martha wrote will reflect the relationships that you noticed in the evaluated expressions.

2. Roger was writing a report about Alpha Centauri, the star closest to the Sun. He learned that it is 4.37 light years away from the Sun and that a light year is about 5.9×10^{12} international miles.

   a. Determine the distance between the Sun and Alpha Centauri in international miles. Write your answer in scientific notation. Show your work.

   b. Explain why it is helpful to express your answer in scientific notation.

   c. Write the distance between the Sun and Alpha Centauri in standard form.

   d. Show with examples why using scientific notation is helpful when comparing very large or very small numbers.

Big Ideas Math Blue **123**
Assessment Book

Chapter 10 Alternative Assessment Rubric

Score	Conceptual Understanding	Mathematical Skills	Work Habits
4	Shows complete understanding of: • multiplying and dividing expressions with exponents • scientific notation and standard form	Evaluates all expressions correctly. Describes all relationships among the expressions. Correctly expresses distance using scientific notation and uses examples to explain usefulness of scientific notation.	Answers all parts of both questions. All calculations are done carefully. All work is neat and well organized.
3	Shows nearly complete understanding of: • multiplying and dividing expressions with exponents • scientific notation and standard form	Evaluates almost all expressions correctly. Describes some relationships among the expressions. Correctly expresses distance using scientific notation and uses an example to explain usefulness of scientific notation.	Answers almost all parts of both questions. Most of the calculations are done carefully. Most of the work is neat and well organized.
2	Shows some understanding of: • multiplying and dividing expressions with exponents • scientific notation and standard form	Evaluates some expressions correctly. Describes one relationship among the expressions. Correctly calculates distance but does not use scientific notation correctly and does not use examples to explain usefulness of scientific notation.	Answers some parts of both questions. Some calculations are done carefully. Some work is neat and well organized.
1	Shows little understanding of: • multiplying and dividing expressions with exponents • scientific notation and standard form	Evaluates few or no expressions correctly. Does not find relationships among the expressions. Does not determine distance and does not explain usefulness of scientific notation.	Answers few parts of both questions. No calculations are done carefully. All work is sloppy and disorganized.

Test 1 **End-of-Course Test**

Solve.

Answers

1. $x - 7 = -13$

2. $15 - 3c = 3$

1. _____

3. One cell phone plan charges $20 per month plus $0.15 per minute used. A second cell phone plan charges $35 per month plus $0.10 per minute used. Write and solve an equation to find the number of minutes you must talk to have the same cost for both calling plans.

2. _____

3. _____

_____

4. **a.** Write the formula for the area of a triangle.

b. Solve the formula for h.

c. The area of a triangle is 36 square inches. Use the new formula to find the height of the triangle in inches and in centimeters.

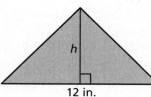

12 in.

4. a._____

b._____

c._____

_____

In Exercises 5 and 6, use the following information.

Parallelograms $ABCD$ and $EFGH$ are congruent.

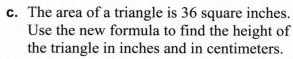

5. _____

6. _____

7. _____

5. Which side of $EFGH$ is congruent to side AD?

6. Find the measure of $\angle E$.

7. A triangle has vertices $A(-1, 3)$, $B(0, 2)$, and $C(-4, 0)$. Find the coordinates of the triangle after translating it up 2 units and reflecting it in the x-axis.

8. _____

_____

_____

_____

_____

9. _____

_____

8. The two figures are similar. Find the values of x and y, and the ratios (larger to smaller) of the perimeters and areas.

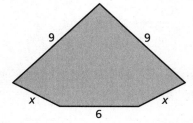

9. An original piece of artwork is 3 feet by 2.5 feet. A reprint of the artwork is 6 inches by 5 inches. Are the pieces similar? If so, what is the ratio of their corresponding side lengths?

Name _____ Date _____

10. Use the figure to find the measure of ∠1.

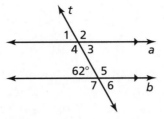

11. Find the measure of each angle of a regular polygon with 8 sides.

12. You want to determine if two triangles are similar. What is the minimum number of angles you need to measure to determine if the triangles are similar? Explain.

Find the slope and the *y*-intercept of the graph of the linear equation. Then sketch its graph.

13. $y = 3x - 2$

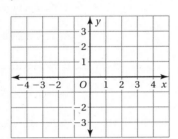

14. $2x + 4y = 6$

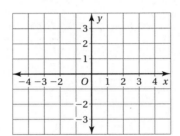

15. The equation $5x + 2y = 20$ represents the cost for a family to attend a play where x is the number of adults and y is the number of children. Find the intercepts and interpret the meaning of each one.

Write an equation of the line in slope-intercept form.

16. the line passing through $(0, 1)$ and $(-4, 5)$

17. the line with slope -2.5 and passing through $(2, 1.5)$

18. Recall that $0°C = 32°F$ and $100°C = 212°F$.

    a. Using x for degrees Celsius and y for degrees Fahrenheit, find an equation of the line passing through $(0, 32)$ and $(100, 212)$.

    b. What is the slope of the line? Explain what the slope means in terms of degrees Celsius and degrees Fahrenheit.

    c. What is the *y*-intercept of the line? Explain what the *y*-intercept means in terms of degrees Celsius and degrees Fahrenheit.

Answers

10. _____

11. _____

12. _____

    _____

    _____

13. _____

    _____

    See left.

14. _____

    _____

    See left.

15. _____

    _____

    _____

    _____

16. _____

17. _____

18. **a.** _____

    b. _____

    _____

    _____

    c. _____

    _____

    _____

Name_____ Date _____

Solve the system.

Answers

19. $y = 3x + 4$
$y - x = 2$

20. $y - 4x = 3$
$2y = 8x + 5$

21. $y = \dfrac{1}{2}x - 1$
$3x - y = -4$

19. _____

20. _____

21. _____

22. It costs $0.05 to send a text message and $0.10 to send a picture on your cell phone. You spend $4 and send five more text messages than pictures. How many text messages x and pictures y did you send?

22. _____

_____

23. Draw a mapping diagram of the set of ordered pairs.

$(2, 3), (3, 5), (4, 1), (5, 2)$

23. _____See left._____

24. The table shows the cost y (in dollars) of x cold drinks.

Drinks, **x**	0	2	4	6
Cost, **y**	0	3	6	9

a. Graph the data.

b. Write a linear function that relates y to x.

c. How much does it cost to buy three drinks?

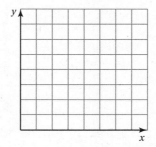

24. a. _____See left._____

b. _____

c. _____

25. _____

26. _____

27. _____

28. _____

29. _____

30. _____

Does the equation or table represent a *linear* or *nonlinear* function?

25. $2x - 4y = 6$

26.

x	3	7	11	15
y	2	4	8	16

Evaluate the expression.

27. $-\sqrt{121} + 15$

28. $6 - 5\sqrt[3]{\dfrac{1}{125}}$

29. A ladder is placed against the side of a house. The top of the ladder is 12 feet above the ground. The base of the ladder is 5 feet away from the house. Find the length of the ladder.

30. What two integers is $\sqrt{42}$ between? Explain.

Test 1 **End-of-Course Test** (continued)

Find the volume of the solid. Round your answer to the nearest tenth.

31.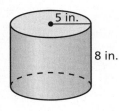
5 in.
8 in.

32.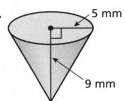
5 mm
9 mm

33.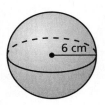
6 cm

34. The table shows the number of years of college education and hourly earnings (in dollars) for several people.

Number of Years, x	0	1	3	5	6
Hourly Earnings, y	6	8	15	25	30

   a. Make a scatter plot of the data.

   b. Draw a line of fit.

   c. Write an equation for the line of fit.

   d. Predict the hourly earnings for a person with four years of college education.

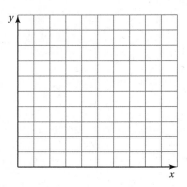

Answers

31. _____

32. _____

33. _____

34. a. __See left.__

   b. __See left.__

   c. _____

   d. _____

35. __See left.__

36. __See left.__

37. _____

38. _____

39. _____

40. _____

41. _____

Choose an appropriate data display for the situation. Explain your reasoning.

35. the percent of students with 0, 1, 2, or more than 2 siblings

36. the average movie theater ticket price over the last ten years

Evaluate.

37. $\left(3^2\right)^{-1}$ **38.** $12^3 \bullet 12^{-4}$ **39.** $\dfrac{(-7)^6}{(-7)^4}$

Multiply. Write your answer in scientific notation.

40. $\left(4.6 \times 10^{-2}\right) \times \left(1.0 \times 10^{-8}\right)$ **41.** $\left(2.5 \times 10^7\right) \times \left(1.4 \times 10^6\right)$

Test 2 **End-of-Course Test**

Solve.

Answers

1. $r - 3.4 = -5.8$

2. $-1 - 2c = 4$

1. _____

2. _____

3. One cell phone plan charges $17.50 per month plus $0.17 per minute used. A second cell phone plan charges $32 per month plus $0.07 per minute used. Write and solve an equation to find the number of minutes you must talk to have the same cost for both calling plans.

3. _____

_____

4. **a.** Write the formula for the area of a triangle. Then solve for h.

   b. The area of a triangle is 14.4 square inches. Use the new formula to find the height of the triangle in inches and in centimeters.

4. **a.**_____

_____

b._____

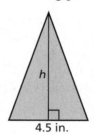

4.5 in.

_____

In Exercises 5 and 6, use the following information.

Parallelograms *ABCD* and *EFGH* are congruent.

5. _____

6. _____

7. _____

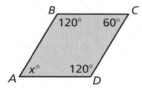 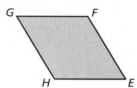

5. Which side of *EFGH* is congruent to side *BC*?

6. Find the measure of $\angle E$.

7. A triangle has vertices $A(-1, 3)$, $B(0, 2)$, and $C(-4, 0)$. Find the coordinates of the triangle after translating it down 3 units and reflecting it in the *y*-axis.

8. The two figures are similar. Find the values of *x* and *y* and the ratios (larger to smaller) of the perimeters and areas.

8. _____

_____

_____

_____

9. _____

_____

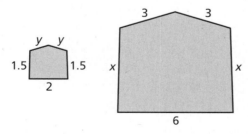

9. An original piece of artwork is 2.75 feet by 2.25 feet. A reprint of the artwork is 22 inches by 18 inches. Are the pieces similar? If so, what is the ratio of their corresponding side lengths?

Test 2 **End-of-Course Test** (continued)

10. Use the figure to find the measure of ∠2.

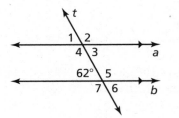

11. Find the measure of each angle of a regular polygon with 10 sides.

12. You want to determine if two triangles are similar. What is the minimum number of angles you need to measure to determine if the triangles are similar? Explain.

Find the slope and the *y*-intercept of the graph of the linear equation. Then sketch its graph.

13. $y = 1.5x + 1$

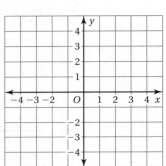

14. $3x + 5y = 1$

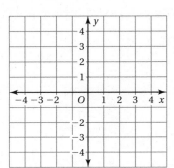

15. The equation $3.5x + 1.5y = 21$ represents the cost for a family to attend a play where *x* is the number of adults and *y* is the number of children. Find the intercepts and interpret the meaning of each one.

Write an equation of the line in slope-intercept form.

16. the line passing through $(0, 2)$ and $(1, -1)$

17. the line with slope -2 and passing through $(3, 1)$

18. Find the value of *x*.

Answers

10. _____

11. _____

12. _____

_____

_____

_____

13. _____

_____

__See left.__

14. _____

_____

__See left.__

15. _____

_____

_____

_____

16. _____

17. _____

18. _____

Name_____ Date_____

Solve the system.

Answers

19. $y = \dfrac{3}{2}x + 2$ **20.** $y - \dfrac{4}{3}x = 2.5$ **21.** $y = \dfrac{1}{2}x - 2$

$\quad\quad y - \dfrac{1}{2}x = \dfrac{1}{2}$ $\quad\quad 3y = 4x - 2$ $\quad\quad x + 2y = 2$

19. _____

20. _____

21. _____

22. It costs $0.07 to send a text message and $0.12 to send a picture on your cell phone. You spend $3.38 and send twice as many text messages as pictures. How many text messages did you send?

22. _____

_____

23. Draw a mapping diagram of the set of ordered pairs.

$(0, 1), (2, 5), (4, 1), (3, 2)$

23. ____See left.____

24. a.___See left.___

b._____

24. The table shows the cost y (in dollars) of x peaches.

Peaches, *x*	0	4	8	12
Cost, *y*	0	3	6	9

a. Graph the data.

b. Write a linear function that relates y to x.

c. What is the cost of six peaches?

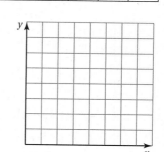

c._____

25. _____

26. _____

27. _____

28. _____

29. _____

30. _____

_____

Does the equation or table represent a *linear* or *nonlinear* function?

25. $\dfrac{2}{3}x - \dfrac{1}{2}y = 4$ **26.**

x	1.5	3.5	5.5	7.5
y	1	2	4	8

Evaluate the expression.

27. $-\sqrt{225} + 4.8$ **28.** $3\sqrt[3]{-343} + 8$

29. A ladder is placed against the side of a house. The top of the ladder is 24 feet above the ground. The base of the ladder is 7 feet away from the house. Find the length of the ladder.

30. What two integers is $-\sqrt{42}$ between? Explain.

Test 2 **End-of-Course Test** (continued)

Find the volume of the solid. Round your answer to the nearest tenth. *Answers*

31.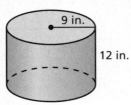

32.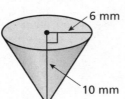

33.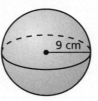

31. _____

32. _____

33. _____

34. a. __See left.__

b. __See left.__

c. _____

d. _____

35. __See left.__

36. __See left.__

37. _____

38. _____

39. _____

40. _____

41. _____

34. The table shows the number of years of college education and hourly earnings (in dollars) for several people.

Number of Years, x	0	1	3	5	6
Hourly Earnings, y	6	9	15	26	31

a. Make a scatter plot of the data.

b. Draw a line of fit.

c. Write an equation for the line of fit.

d. Predict the hourly earnings for a person with four years of college education.

Choose an appropriate data display for the situation. Explain your reasoning.

35. the percent of students who chose red, green, blue, yellow, or another color as their favorite color

36. the average cost of a movie ticket over the last twenty years

Evaluate.

37. $\left(-3^3\right)^{-1}$

38. $12^{27} \cdot 12^{-29}$

39. $\dfrac{(-6)^7}{(-6)^5}$

Multiply. Write your answer in scientific notation.

40. $\left(4.0 \times 10^{-1}\right) \times \left(2.5 \times 10^{-4}\right)$

41. $\left(6.0 \times 10^{-5}\right) \times \left(1.5 \times 10^{-13}\right)$

Name_____ Date _____

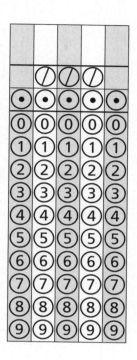

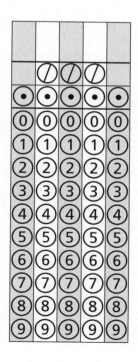

Resource **Gridded Response Answer Sheet**

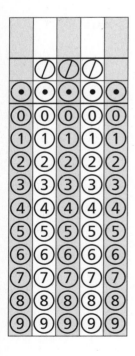

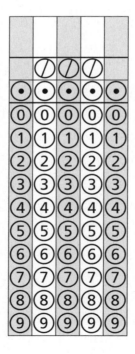

Answers

Pre-Course Test

1. no   **2.** yes

3. yes   **4.** $0.08 per ounce

5. $-6, -|4|, -2, |-5|, 6$ **6.** $-8.5, -\dfrac{42}{5}, \dfrac{15}{2}, 10.2$

7. $x < 6$ **8.** $x \geq 4$ **9.** 60 cm^3

10. 50 mi   **11.** 7   **12.** -15

13. 56   **14.** -15 **15.** 34

16. 41   **17.** -238 **18.** 31

19. $\dfrac{37}{45}$ **20.** $-\dfrac{7}{6}$ or $-1\dfrac{1}{6}$

21. $\dfrac{13}{50}$ **22.** $-\dfrac{17}{24}$ **23.** 0.36

24. -44.361 **25.** -2.54 **26.** $4 : 1$

27. $x = -9$ **28.** $x = -5$ **29.** $x = 6$

30. $x = -1$ **31.** $x = 2$ **32.** $x = -7$

33. $6x + 3 - 3 = 27 - 3$ Subtraction Prop. of Equality

        $\dfrac{6x}{3} = \dfrac{24}{3}$ Division Prop. of Equality

        $2x = 8$

34. $(-2, 3)$ **35.** $(-1, -4)$ **36.** $(1, 4)$

37. $(3, -2)$ **38.** $=$ **39.** $>$

40. $<$ **41.** 0.75   **42.** 0.3125   **43.** 5.25

44. no; This sample favors people who like to wear red.

45.

Stem	Leaf
7	6 7 7 8 9
8	0 2 2 4 4 7
9	0 5 7
10	0

       Key: 7 | 6 = 76

46. $\dfrac{4}{11}$

Chapter 1

1.1–1.2 Quiz

1. $c = 4\dfrac{1}{3}$ **2.** $x = -2$ **3.** $s = 1.2$

4. $r = 4$ **5.** $d = 9$ **6.** $m = 13\dfrac{1}{3}$

7. $n = 0$ **8.** $q = 8$

9. $x = 150$; $50°, 130°, 40°, 140°$

10. $x = 160$; $80°, 80°, 145°, 100°, 135°$

11. $13   **12.** 15 ft, 30 ft, 45 ft, 60 ft

13. $360 = 60t$; 6 h   **14.** $\dfrac{29 + c}{4} = 10$; 11 cars

1.3–1.4 Quiz

1. $p = -4$ **2.** $y = 0$ **3.** $k = -\dfrac{1}{3}$

4. $r = 22$ **5.** no solution

6. infinitely many solutions

7. $y = \dfrac{5}{4}x - \dfrac{5}{2}$ **8.** $y = 3x - 7$

9. $h = \dfrac{3V}{\pi r^2}$ **10.** $b = \dfrac{2A}{h}$

11. at your school   **12.** $h = \dfrac{2A}{b + B}$; 16 ft

13. Route that passes the mall: 11 miles
     Route that passes the theater: 13 miles

14. $h = \dfrac{S - 2\pi r^2}{2\pi r}$

Test A

1. $y = 21$ **2.** $x = 6$ **3.** $p = 7$

4. $x = -3$ **5.** $w = 18$ **6.** $q = -2$

7. no solution

8. infinitely many solutions

9. infinitely many solutions

10. no solution

11. $y = 3 - \dfrac{2}{5}x$ **12.** $y = \dfrac{4}{3} - \dfrac{1}{2}x$

13. $y = 0.5x - 2$ **14.** $y = 8x + 20$

15. a. $R = P + C$ **b.** $870

16. $h = \dfrac{V}{w\ell}$ **17.** $p = s + 0.2t$

Answers

18. $s = \dfrac{Z}{L}$ **19.** $T = \dfrac{PV}{nR}$

20. $x = 25$; $60°$, $75°$, $45°$

21. $x = 75$; $70°$, $105°$, $75°$, $110°$

22. $160 = g + 24$; $g = 136$; 136 students

23. $5x = 12.50$; $x = 2.5$; 2.5 h

24. $395 = 24n + 35$; $24n = 360$; $n = 15$; 15 birthday cakes

25. 156 in.

26. no; The equation that results from setting the amounts paid equal has no solution.

27. a. $B = \dfrac{2A}{h} - b$ **b.** 28 in.

Test B

1. $d = 14$ **2.** $x = \dfrac{11}{15}$ **3.** $s = -\pi$

4. $w = -15$ **5.** $a = -1$ **6.** $g = \dfrac{2}{3}$

7. no solution

8. infinitely many solutions

9. infinitely many solutions

10. no solution   **11.** $y = \dfrac{5}{3}x - \dfrac{2\pi}{3}$

12. $y = 1.6x - 2$ **13.** $y = 1.5x + 0.5$

14. $y = -\dfrac{1}{2}x + \dfrac{3}{2}$ **15. a.** $P = \dfrac{I}{rt}$ **b.** \$500

16. $c = \dfrac{3i}{e}$ **17.** $w = \dfrac{P}{2} - \ell$

18. $R = \dfrac{V}{I}$ **19.** $h = \dfrac{S - 3\pi r^2}{2\pi r}$

20. $x = 43$; $129°$, $86°$, $90°$, $55°$

21. $x = 60$; $144°$, $78°$, $120°$, $120°$, $78°$

22. $c + 11.50 = 47$; $c = 35.50$; \$35.50

23. $3.50x = 31.50$; $x = 9$; 9 video games

24. $5x + 8.50 = 38.45$; $x = 5.99$; \$5.99

25. a. $p = \dfrac{C}{1.06}$ **b.** \$59

26. no; The equation that results from setting the areas equal has no solution; yes; $x = 3$

27. a. $h = \dfrac{3V}{\pi r^2}$ **b.** height

Alternative Assessment

1. a. *Sample answer:* Let x be the number.

$$7x + 2 = 2x + 7$$
$$5x = 5$$
$$x = 1$$

Equation to show why it always works:

$$ax + b = bx + a$$
$$ax - bx = a - b$$
$$(a - b)x = a - b$$
$$x = 1$$

b. *Sample answer:*

$$\dfrac{4x + 8}{4} = n$$
$$x + 2 = n$$
$$x = n - 2$$

To find the original number choice, subtract 2 from the number given to you.

Chapter 2

2.1–2.4 Quiz

1. congruent; The corresponding sides are congruent.

2. not congruent; The corresponding sides are not congruent.

3. yes   **4.** no   **5.** no   **6.** yes

7. *Sample answer:* 1) rotate $90°$ counterclockwise about the origin, translate 1 unit down; 2) translate 1 unit left, rotate $90°$ counterclockwise about the origin

8. *Sample answer:* 1) rotate $90°$ counterclockwise about the origin, translate 2 units right and 2 units down; 2) translate 2 units left and 2 units down, rotate $270°$ clockwise about the origin

9. $A'(-4, 2)$, $B'(-2, -1)$, $C'(2, 2)$

10. $W'(1, -2)$, $X'(-1, -1)$, $Y'(-2, -2)$, $Z'(-1, -3)$

2.5–2.7 Quiz

1. yes; Corresponding side lengths are proportional and corresponding angles have the same measure.

Answers

2. $x = 12$ **3.** $x = 7.5$ **4.** $\dfrac{4}{3}; \dfrac{16}{9}$ **5.** $\dfrac{5}{9}; \dfrac{25}{81}$

6. yes   **7.** no   **8.** 216 in.^{2}

9. $A'(-2, -1)$, $B'(-2, 2)$, $C'(3, 2)$

Test A

1. $\angle B$ **2.** $\angle Q$ **3.** side CA **4.** rotation

5. translation   **6.** dilation   **7.** reflection

8. $A'(2, 0)$, $B'(5, 0)$, $C'(5, 2)$, and $D'(2, 2)$

9. $X'(-1, 5)$, $Y'(3, 5)$, $Z'(-1, -1)$

10.

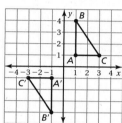

$A'(-1, -1)$, $B'(-1, -4)$, and $C'(-3, -1)$

11. no; The corresponding side lengths are not proportional.

12. yes; Corresponding side lengths are proportional and corresponding angles have the same measure.

13. $\dfrac{3}{8}; \dfrac{9}{64}$ **14.** $\dfrac{3}{5}; \dfrac{9}{25}$ **15.** $\dfrac{1}{3}$

16. a. 7 units to the right, 5 units up

   b. $(3, -3)$ **c.** $(2, -4)$

17. 7 in.   **18.** 4.5 in.^{2}

Test B

1. side EH **2.** 4   **3.** 4 cm

4. 9 cm   **5.** reflection   **6.** rotation

7. dilation   **8.** translation

9. $X'(-2, 3)$, $Y'(-1, 3)$, $Z'(-1, 1)$

10.

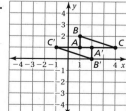

$A'(2, 1)$, $B'(2, 0)$, and $C'(-1, 1)$

11. $x = 8$ **12.** $x = 35$ **13.** false   **14.** true

15. a. rotation   **b.** reflection   **c.** dilation

   d. Design A and Design G, Design H and Design C

   e. Design F

16. If k is less than 1, then it is a reduction. If k is greater than 1, then it is an enlargement.

17. 81 ft^2 **18.** 36 cm

Alternative Assessment

1. a.

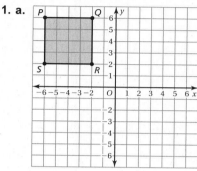

   b. $(2, 6)$, $(6, 6)$, $(6, 2)$, $(2, 2)$

   c. $(2, -2)$, $(6, -2)$, $(6, -6)$, $(2, -6)$

   d. $(-6, -2)$, $(-2, -2)$, $(-2, -6)$, $(-6, -6)$

   e. reflection of $PQRS$ in the x-axis or translate $PQRS$ 8 units down

   f. The image in part (b) could have been made by translating $PQRS$ 8 units right. The image in part (c) could have been made by translating $PQRS$ 8 units right and 8 units down, or by rotating $PQRS$ 180° about the origin. The image in part (d) could have been made by translating $PQRS$ 8 units down.

2. a–c.

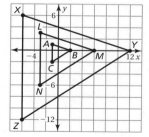

   b. reduction; $\dfrac{1}{3}$ **c.** enlargement

   d. enlargement; 6; reduction; $\dfrac{1}{6}$; The scale factors are reciprocals of each other.

Answers

Chapter 3

3.1–3.2 Quiz

1. 85°; *Sample answer:* ∠6 and the given angle are supplementary, and ∠6 and ∠3 are alternate interior angles.

2. 95°; ∠5 and the given angle are vertical angles.

3. 85°; ∠6 and the given angle are supplementary.

4. 85°; *Sample answer:* ∠1 and the given angle are alternate exterior angles, and ∠1 and ∠2 are supplementary.

5. 46°; ∠6 and ∠3 are alternate interior angles.

6. 102°; ∠5 and ∠8 are vertical angles.

7. 82°; *Sample answer:* ∠4 and ∠5 are alternate interior angles, and ∠5 and ∠7 are supplementary.

8. 121°; *Sample answer:* ∠4 and ∠3 are supplementary, and ∠6 and ∠3 are alternate interior angles.

9. 110°; 35°; 35°   10. 85°; 63°; 32°

11. 39°; 39°; 102°   12. 150°

13. 75°

14. ∠1 = 112°, ∠2 = 68°; The 68° angle is supplementary to ∠1 and congruent to its corresponding ∠2.

15. Exterior angle with wall: $180 - 7(5) = 145°$;
    Exterior angle with ground: $180 - 11(5) = 125°$;
    $7x + 11x + 90 = 180$
    $x = 5$

3.3–3.4 Quiz

1. 900°   2. 1260°

3. 96°; 84°; 146°; 112°; 102°

4. 106°; 120°; 102°; 224°; 114°; 121°; 113°

5. 92°; 62°; 100°; 200°; 86°

6. 106°; 128°; 126°   7. 118°; 34°; 118°; 90°

8. no; The triangles do not have the same angle measures.

9. yes; The triangles have the same angle measures, 31°, 43°, and 106°.

10. 31 sides

11. a. Angles B and D are right angles, so they are congruent. Angles ACB and ECD are vertical angles, so they are congruent. Because two angles in $\triangle ABC$ are congruent to two angles in $\triangle ECD$, the third angles are also congruent and the triangles are similar.

    b. 175 ft

Test A

1. 152°; The angles are vertical angles.

2. 152°; The angles are corresponding angles.

3. 152°; The angles are alternate exterior angles.

4. 28°; *Sample answer:* ∠3 is supplementary to 152° and ∠3 and ∠6 are alternate interior angles.

5. 13°, 13°, 154°   6. 60°, 60°, 60°

7. 143°   8. 134°

9. 48°, 132°, 48°, 132°

10. 90°, 90°, 135°, 135°, 135°, 135°

11. 75°, 90°, 90°, 105°   12. 114°, 120°, 126°

13. yes; $x = 69$, so the triangles have the same angle measures and they are similar.

14. no; $b = 47$ and $c = 42$, so the triangles do not have the same angle measures.

15. *Sample answer:*
    1. Use the congruence of the corresponding angles ∠8 and the 114° angle, and the fact that ∠8 and ∠7 are supplementary.
    2. Use the congruence of the alternate interior angles ∠5 and the 114° angle, and the fact that ∠5 and ∠7 are supplementary.

16. no; The sum of the angle measures must be 720°, not 710°.

17. 2000 ft

Test B

1. 84°; The angles are alternate exterior angles.

2. 96°; *Sample answer:* ∠6 and ∠5 are supplementary, so ∠5 = 180° − 84° = 96°.

3. 84°; The 84° angle and ∠4 are corresponding angles.

Answers

4. 96°; The 84° angle is supplementary to ∠3, and ∠3 and ∠7 are corresponding angles.

5. 16°, 39°, 125°

6. 45°, 45°, 90°

7. 93°

8. 137°

9. 1800°

10. 720°

11. 88.5°, 100°, 105°, 98°, 175°, 142°, 106°, 265.5°

12. 60°, 85°, 120°, 101°, 174°

13. 63°, 83°, 105°, 109°

14. 62°, 30°, 80°, 90°, 98°

15. no; $x = 43$ and $y = 91$, so the triangles have different angle measures.

16. 20°

17. 161°

18. 250 ft

Alternative Assessment

1. a. *Sample answer:* ∠AHC and ∠FHE, ∠BGC and ∠HGD; Vertical angles are formed when two lines intersect.

   b. *Sample answer:* ∠HGD and ∠FHE, ∠BGC and ∠AHG; Corresponding angles are formed by a transversal intersecting parallel lines.

   c. *Sample answer:* ∠GDC and ∠GDE, ∠BGC and ∠HGB; The angles form a straight line, which is 180°.

   d. *Sample answer:* ∠BAH and ∠HAF, ∠BCG and ∠GCD; Two angles whose measures have a sum of 90° are complementary.

   e. *Sample answer:* ∠BGH and ∠GHE, ∠HGD and ∠AHG; Alternate interior angles are formed when a transversal intersects two parallel lines.

2. ∠CFE has a measure of 59° because it has the same angle measure as ∠FEH, and that angle measure is equal to 90° − 31°, or 59°.

   ∠AHC has a measure of 62° because it is equal to the vertical angle ∠FHE, which is equal to 180° − 2(59°) = 62°.

   ∠CGD has a measure of 118° because it is supplementary to ∠FGD, which is corresponding angles with ∠FHE, which is 62°, and 180° − 62° = 118°.

3. *Sample answer:* △AHC is similar to △BGC and △CEA is similar to △CDB; side measures of △AHC: $AH = HC = 5$ units and $AC = 6$ units; side measures of △BGC: $BG = GC = 2.5$ units and $BC = 3$ units; side measures of △CEA: $CE = 8$ units, $CA = 6$ units, and $AE = 10$ units; side measures of △CBD: $CD = 4$ units, $CB = 3$ units, and $BD = 5$ units

Chapter 4

4.1–4.3 Quiz

1.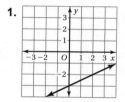

2.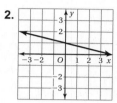

3. $\dfrac{4}{5}$

4. $-\dfrac{1}{3}$

5. $-\dfrac{5}{4}$

6.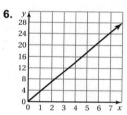

The slope indicates that the unit cost is $3.50 per pound.

7. a. $y = \dfrac{3}{2}x$

   b. The slope indicates that the recipe uses 3 cups of flour for every 2 eggs.

   c. 8 eggs

4.4–4.7 Quiz

1. slope: −4; y-intercept: −6

2. slope: $\dfrac{1}{2}$; y-intercept: $-\dfrac{1}{3}$

3. x-intercept: 8; y-intercept: −6

4. x-intercept: −2; y-intercept: 4

Answers

5. a.

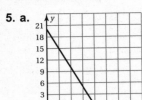

b. The x-intercept shows that you can buy 8 sandwiches if you don't buy any beverages. The y-intercept shows that you can buy 20 beverages if you don't buy any sandwiches.

6. $y = 2x - 1$

7. $y = -\dfrac{1}{3}x + 1$

8. $y - 2 = -2(x - 1)$

9. $y + 2 = \dfrac{1}{4}(x - 4)$

10. $y = -1$

11. $y = 2x + 1$

12. $y = -2x + 10$

Test A

1. *Sample answer:*

x	0	4
$y = \dfrac{1}{2}x$	0	2

Sample answer: $(2, 1)$

2. *Sample answer:*

x	1	-1
$y = x + 3$	4	2

Sample answer: $(0, 3)$

Graph for Exercises 1 and 2

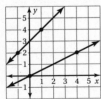

3. $y = -\dfrac{1}{4}x - 3$

4. $y = \dfrac{2}{3}x - 1$

5. 0

6. $\dfrac{1}{2}$

7. the sliding pole; $\dfrac{5}{3} > \dfrac{3}{2}$

8. *Sample answer:* $y = 2x + 1$

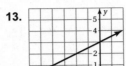

9. $3; -6$

10. $-\dfrac{3}{4}; -5$

11. $\dfrac{7}{9}; -3\dfrac{1}{3}$

12. The y-intercept, -12, is the depth (12 m) at which the submarine starts at time 0. The slope -8 is the speed at which it descends, -8 m/min.

13. 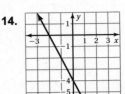   **14.**

15. a. $6x + y = 9$

   b. 9; the distance from home at which you start at time 0

   c. $1\dfrac{1}{2}$; the time after which you arrive home, in hours

16. $y = \dfrac{3}{2}x + 1$

17. $y = x + 4$

18. $y = -2x + 1$

19. $y = -\dfrac{1}{2}x + 9$

20. a. $\dfrac{4}{5}$; The kite rises 4 feet every 5 seconds (or the kite rises 0.8 feet per second).

   b. $y = \dfrac{4}{5}x + 4$

   c. 16 ft

   d. When you first let out the string, the height of the kite is 4 feet.

Test B

1. $y = -\dfrac{3}{2}x - 2$ **2.** $y = \dfrac{3}{4}x + 1$

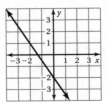

3. 2

4. $\dfrac{1}{3}$

5. the first hill; $\dfrac{2}{10} > \dfrac{2}{15}$

Answers

6. The top and middle lines have the same slope, $\frac{2}{3}$, and are therefore parallel. The bottom line has a slope of $\frac{3}{4}$.

7. -2; -1 **8.** $\frac{1}{3}$; 0 **9.** $\frac{3}{4}$; -2

10. The x-intercept is the x-coordinate of the point where $y = 0$. Substitute 0 for y in the equation and solve. The x-intercept is $\frac{1}{2}$.

11. x-intercept, 2;   **12.** x-intercept, -1;
y-intercept, -3 y-intercept, 2

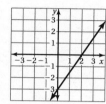 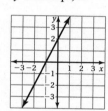

13. a. $15x + y = 90$

    b. 90; the amount owed at the start when $x = 0$

    c. 6; the number of weeks needed to reduce the amount owed to 0

14. $y = \frac{2}{3}x$ **15.** $y = 3$

16. $y = \frac{5}{2}x + 7$ **17.** $y = -3x + 22$

18. a. -5; The temperature drops $5°F$ every 1000 feet.

    b. $y = -5x + 75$

    c. The x-intercept is 15. The temperature is $0°F$ at an altitude of 15,000 feet.

    d. $20°F$

Alternative Assessment

1. a. $2.5t + 5m = 20$

    b.

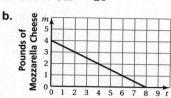

Pounds of Tomatoes

    The m-intercept shows that Sophia can buy 4 pounds of mozzarella cheese if she doesn't buy any tomatoes. The t-intercept shows that Sophia can buy 8 pounds of tomatoes if she doesn't buy any mozzarella cheese.

    c. She can buy 6 pounds of tomatoes and 1 pound of cheese, 4 pounds of tomatoes and 2 pounds of cheese, or 2 pounds of tomatoes and 3 pounds of cheese.

    d. She bought 4 pounds of tomatoes and 2 pounds of mozzarella cheese.

2. a. 1.5

    b. The tree grows at a rate of 1.5 feet per year.

    c. $h = 1.5t + 3$

    d. 48 feet

    e. 38 years

    f. The graph would have a steeper slope.

Chapter 5

5.1–5.2 Quiz

1. A; $(2, 3)$ **2.** B; $(2, -3)$

3. $(-4, 2)$ **4.** $(-4, -1)$

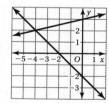 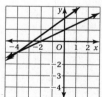

5. $(-2, -1)$ **6.** $(1, 2)$

7. $(12, 6)$ **8.** 15 boys; 25 girls

9. length $= 13$ feet; width $= 5$ feet

5.3–5.4 Quiz

1. $(-4, 2)$ **2.** $(1, -7)$ **3.** $(-6, 3)$

4. infinitely many solutions

Answers

5. no solution

6. $(-3, 0)$

7. $x = 1$

8. $x = 2$

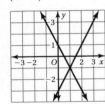

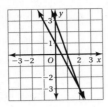

9. no; The system of equations for the situation has infinitely many solutions, so you cannot determine the cost per pound of each meat.

10. a. $16s + 10u = 400$
$s + u = 28$

   b. 20 scented candles; 8 unscented candles

Test A

1. B; $(1, 1)$

2. A; $(-1, -1)$

3. $(1, -1)$

4. $(1, 3)$

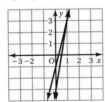

5. $(3, 5)$

6. $(1, 7)$

7. $(-3, 1)$

8. 19 red marbles, 8 blue marbles

9. 36 apples, 24 oranges

10. $(1, -3)$

11. $(-20, 2)$

12. $(30, 10)$

13. infinitely many solutions; The two equations are equivalent.

14. no solution; The two equations represent lines with the same slope but different y-intercepts.

15. one solution; The two equations represent lines with different slopes. Because the two lines have different slopes, they are not parallel and must intersect at a point.

16. $x = -1$

17. $x = -1$

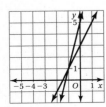

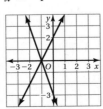

18. no solution

19. $x = 1$

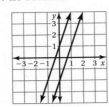

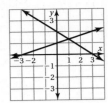

20. $6

21. no; The system of equations that represents the situation has no solution, so you cannot determine the prices of taco salads and iced tea.

Test B

1. $(-3, 0)$

2. $(3, 3)$

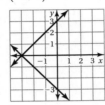

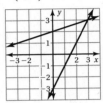

3. $(1, 1)$

4. $(3, 1)$

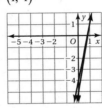

5. $(3, 6)$

6. $(1, 6)$

7. $(-3, 3)$

8. 20 red pens; 4 blue pens

9. 15 orange fish; 16 red fish

10. $110°$; $70°$

11. $(-1, -5)$

12. $(4, 10)$

13. $(-1, -8)$

14. one solution; The two equations represent lines with different slopes. Because the two lines have different slopes, they are not parallel and must intersect at a point.

15. infinitely many solutions; The two equations are equivalent.

16. no solution; The two equations represent lines with the same slope but different y-intercepts.

Answers

17. $x = 2$

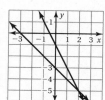

18. $x = -1$

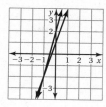

19. infinitely many solutions

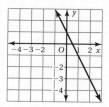

20. $x = -\dfrac{3}{2}$

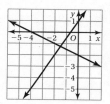

21. $16

22. no; The system of equations that represents the situation has an infinite number of solutions, so the weight of each container cannot be determined.

Alternative Assessment

1. a.

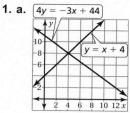

The solution to the system of linear equations is $(4, 8)$.

b. *Sample answer:* I drew a line that passed through both the origin and $(4, 8)$.

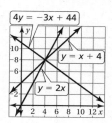

c. $y = 2x$

d. *Sample answer:* $y = 6x - 16$; $y = -2x + 16$

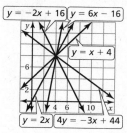

e. *Sample answer:*

$y = x + 4$

$8 \overset{?}{=} 4 + 4$

$8 = 8$

$4y = -3x + 44$

$4(8) \overset{?}{=} -3(4) + 44$

$32 \overset{?}{=} -12 + 44$

$32 = 32$

$y = 2x$

$8 \overset{?}{=} (2)4$

$8 = 8$

$y = 6x - 16$

$8 \overset{?}{=} 6(4) - 16$

$8 \overset{?}{=} 24 - 16$

$8 = 8$

$y = -2x + 16$

$8 \overset{?}{=} -2(4) + 16$

$8 \overset{?}{=} 8 + 16$

$8 = 8$

f. *Sample answer:* equations used: $y = 2x$ and $y = x + 4$; Yolanda says she has twice as many T-shirts as her younger brother, Xavier. Xavier said that she only has 4 more than he does. How many T-shirts do Yolanda and Xavier have?

Answers

2. a. *Sample answer:* Both equations are linear and both are in the same variables, so they form a system of linear equations.

b.
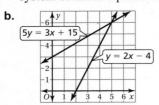

The solution is $(5, 6)$.

$$2x - 4 = \frac{3}{5}x + 3$$

$$\frac{7}{5}x = 7$$

$$x = 5$$

$$y = 2x - 4$$

$$= 2(5) - 4$$

$$= 10 - 4$$

$$= 6$$

The solution is $(5, 6)$.

c. *Sample answer:* The slope of $y = 2x - 4$ is 2.

The slope of $5y = 3x + 15$ is $\frac{3}{5}$. To find slope on the graph, find the ratio of rise over run by counting the number of units y changes between two points, and the number of units x changes. To find slope in an equation, when the equation is solved for y, the coefficient of x is the slope.

d. The x- intercept of $y = 2x - 4$ is 2 and the y-intercept is -4. The x- intercept of $5y = 3x + 15$ is -5 and the y-intercept is 3.

To find these values graphically, examine the graphs to see where the line for the equation crosses the y-axis to find the y-intercept and where it crosses the x-axis to find the x-intercept. To find these values algebraically, find the value of y when x is zero to find the y-intercept and find the value of x when y is zero to find the x-intercept.

e. $2x - y = 4$; $3x - 5y = -15$

Chapter 6

6.1–6.3 Quiz

1. $(2, 3), (6, 4), (8, 11), (10, 4)$; function

2. $(7, -13), (9, -9), (11, -5), (14, -1)$; function

3. -9 **4.** 2   **5.** $y = -5x$

6. $y = 2x - 3$ **7.** $y = -\frac{1}{2}x + 4$

8. a. $g = -\frac{1}{20}m + 20$ **b.** 14 gallons

6.4–6.5 Quiz

1. linear; The graph is a straight line.

2. nonlinear; The graph is not a straight line.

3. linear; The graph is a straight line.

4. nonlinear; The graph is not a straight line.

5. The sales rate of the tickets increase at a constant rate, then stay constant, then increase at a constant rate.

6. Speed increases at an increasing rate then increases at a decreasing rate.

7. Ounces increase at an decreasing rate.

8. The amount of the account increases at a constant rate, then decreases instantly, then increases at a constant rate.

9. nonlinear; As t increases by 1, v increases by different amounts.

Test A

1. $(0, 4), (1, 6), (2, 8), (3, 10), (4, 12)$

2. $(1, -3), (3, -1), (5, -8), (7, -9), (9, -9)$

3. $y = 4$ **4.** $y = -28$ **5.** $y = 5x$

6. $y = x - 4$;

Input, x	1	2	3	4
Output, y	-3	-2	-1	0

7. $y = 2x + 2$ **8.** $y = 4x$

9.
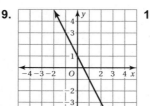

10.
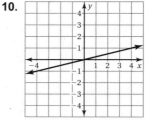

Answers

11. nonlinear; The graph is not a line.

12. linear; The graph is a line.

13. nonlinear; The graph is not a line.

14. linear; The graph is a line.

15. 24

16. The usage decreases at a decreasing rate.

Test B

1. Input, x Output, y **2.** Input, x Output, y

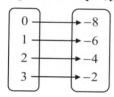 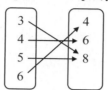

3. a. Input, x Output, y

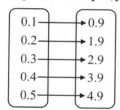

b. 6.9; Following the pattern in the table, the speed for 0.6 second is 5.9 meters per second and the speed for 0.7 second is 6.9 meters per second.

4. $y = x - 2$ **5.** $y = \frac{1}{3}x$ **6.** $x = 8$

7. $x = -1$ **8.** $E = 8h$; $320

9.   **10.**

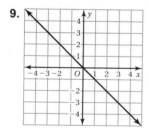

11. $y = x + 1$ **12.** $y = -\frac{x}{2}$

13. a. $y = 15x$ **b.** 5 boxes

14. for Car A

15. nonlinear; The graph is not a line.

16. linear; The graph is a line.

17. 52

18. a. the graph of female height; *Sample answer:* If the length of the femur increases 1 inch, the male graph rises 2.2 inches and the female graph rises 2.3 inches.

b. male: 60 in.; female: 58.5 in.

c. 20 in.

Alternative Assessment

1. a.   Lou   Gene
    Input, x Output, y Input, x Output, y

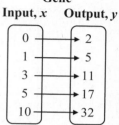 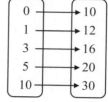

b. Lou: $y = 2x + 10$; Gene: $y = 3x + 2$

c. Lou: 50 DVDs; Gene: 62 DVDs

d.

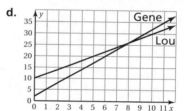

Gene's graph is steeper because he buys 3 DVDs each week and Lou only buys 2 DVDs each week.

e. The intersection point $(8, 26)$ means that after 8 weeks, Lou and Gene each have 26 DVDs.

f. Lou: $2(15) + 10 = 40$; Lou is correct.

Gene: $3(15) + 2 = 47$; Gene is incorrect.

g. $y = 5x + 12$; The missing input is 13 weeks.

h.

Number of weeks, x	0	1	2
Number of DVDs, y	20	24	28

$y = 4x + 20$

Chapter 7

7.1–7.3 Quiz

1. -4 **2.** $\frac{5}{13}$ **3.** ± 3.5

4. 8   **5.** -2 **6.** $\frac{4}{3}$

7. 3   **8.** 0   **9.** $\frac{7}{8}$ **10.** 1006

Answers

11. 25   **12.** 71   **13.** 89 ft   **14.** 3 cm

15. $6\frac{2}{3}$ in.   **16.** 37 yd   **17.** 3 cm   **18.** 11 in.

7.4–7.5 Quiz

1. irrational   **2.** rational

3. natural, whole, integer, rational

4. a. 5   **b.** 4.9   **5. a.** −15   **b.** −14.8

6. a. 2   **b.** 1.9

7. $\frac{1}{9}$; $\frac{1}{9}$ is to the right of $\sqrt{\dfrac{1}{102}} \approx \dfrac{1}{10}$ on a number line.

8. π; Any number greater than 1 is greater than its square root.

9. $2\frac{4}{9}$ **10.** $-3\frac{3}{11}$ **11.** no   **12.** yes

13. 5   **14.** 13   **15.** $\sqrt{34}$ **16.** $2\sqrt{10}$

17. no; The car must travel 13 miles to get back to the ramp and there is only enough gas to travel 12.7 miles.

Test A

1. −9   **2.** $\pm\dfrac{1}{3}$ **3.** −1

4. $-\dfrac{2}{3}$ **5.** 4   **6.** 2.9

7. 6   **8.** 3   **9.** 8 ft

10. 50 m; Because the ratio of areas is 25 to 9, the ratio of side lengths is 5 to 3, or 50 to 30.

11. 24 in.   **12.** 12.5 m

13. 35 ft   **14.** integer, rational

15. irrational   **16.** rational

17. a. 6   **b.** 6.1   **18. a.** −7   **b.** −7.2

19. a. 2   **b.** 1.8   **20.** 21.2 in.

21. 4.5; 4.5 is to the right of $\sqrt{17} \approx 4$ on a number line.

22. $-10\frac{1}{5}$; $-10\frac{1}{5}$ is to the right of $-\sqrt{120} \approx -11$ on a number line.

23. $\dfrac{4}{3}$ **24.** $\dfrac{14}{99}$ **25.** 17   **26.** $\sqrt{89}$

27. no   **28.** yes   **29.** 5.8 units

Test B

1. −13   **2.** ±100   **3.** $\dfrac{4}{9}$ **4.** 100

5. $\dfrac{1}{3}$ **6.** 2.85   **7.** 1.14   **8.** 24

9. $1\frac{3}{4}$ **10.** 12 in.   **11.** 6 ft   **12.** $1\frac{1}{4}$ in.

13. a. 18 cm   **b.** 27 cm

14. rational   **15.** irrational

16. irrational   **17. a.** −7   **b.** −6.8

18. a. 14   **b.** 13.8   **19.** 6.3 sec

20. 2.2; Because $4.4 = 2(2.2)$, $\sqrt{4.4} < 2.2$.

21. −0.8; Because $0.8 < 1$, $\sqrt{0.8} > 0.8$. So, $-\sqrt{0.8} < -0.8$.

22. $\dfrac{37}{99}$ **23.** $7\frac{2}{11}$ **24.** 29

25. 26   **26.** yes   **27.** yes

28. The longest side is 10 units long. Using the Pythagorean Theorem, the shortest side is $\sqrt{4^2 + 2^2} = \sqrt{20}$ units long and the third side is $\sqrt{4^2 + 8^2} = \sqrt{80}$ units long. Because $20 + 80 = 100$, the triangle is a right triangle.

29. 2 in.^{2}

Alternative Assessment

1. a. $\sqrt{90} \approx 9.5$, $\sqrt{909} \approx 30.1$, $\sqrt{9} = 3$, $\sqrt{900} = 30$, $\sqrt{9\pi} = 3\pi \approx 9.4$

b. $\sqrt{9}$, $\sqrt{9\pi}$, $\sqrt{90}$, $\sqrt{900}$, $\sqrt{909}$

c. $\sqrt{9}$: rational; 9 is a perfect square.
$\sqrt{9\pi}$: irrational; π is irrational.
$\sqrt{90}$: irrational; 90 is not a perfect square.
$\sqrt{900}$: rational; 900 is a perfect square.
$\sqrt{909}$: irrational; 909 is not a perfect square.

Answers

2. a. $AB = 4$, $DC = 12$, $BD = 5$, $BC = 13$

   b. *Sample answer:* no; The triangles are not similar because there is not a proportional relationship between the sides. For example, $\dfrac{3}{5} \neq \dfrac{4}{12}$.

Chapter 8

8.1–8.2 Quiz

1. $150\pi \approx 471.2 \text{ mm}^3$ **2.** $800\pi \approx 2513.3 \text{ in.}^3$

3. $16\pi \approx 50.3 \text{ cm}^3$ **4.** $64\pi \approx 201.1 \text{ in.}^3$

5. $\dfrac{251}{8\pi} \approx 10.0 \text{ ft}$ **6.** $\sqrt{\dfrac{85}{3\pi}} \approx 3.0 \text{ yd}$

7. about 6 feet   **8.** 8 times greater

8.3–8.4 Quiz

1. $\dfrac{4000\pi}{3} \approx 4188.8 \text{ cm}^3$ **2.** $\dfrac{62.5\pi}{3} \approx 65.4 \text{ in.}^3$

3. 3 in.   **4.** $\dfrac{3}{4}$ ft   **5.** 96 in.^3

6. no   **7.** $b = 20 \text{ m}$

8. Surface Area $= 310 \text{ ft}^2$

9. about 2212 in.^3 **10.** 9.6 cm^3

Test A

1. $600\pi \approx 1885.0 \text{ in.}^3$ **2.** $12\pi \approx 37.7 \text{ mm}^3$

3. $84\pi \approx 263.9 \text{ in.}^3$ **4.** $48\pi \approx 150.8 \text{ mm}^3$

5. $98.784\pi \approx 310.3 \text{ ft}^3$ **6.** $\dfrac{157.216\pi}{3} \approx 164.6 \text{ ft}^3$

7. $\dfrac{201}{16\pi} \approx h = 4.0 \text{ cm}$ **8.** $\dfrac{79}{25\pi} \approx h = 3.0 \text{ in.}$

9. $\dfrac{1}{2}$ ft   **10.** 2 yd

11. $60\pi \approx 188.5 \text{ cm}^3$ **12.** $24\pi \approx 75.4 \text{ m}^3$

13. yes   **14.** no   **15.** $V = 9604 \text{ ft}^3$

16. $S = 175 \text{ cm}^2$ **17.** 71 gal

18. $18\pi \text{ in.}^3$; Because the cone and cylinder have the same radius and height, the volume of the cone is one third the volume of the cylinder, so the volume of the cylinder is 3 times the volume of the cone.

19. 48 in.

20. $\dfrac{\text{Volume of hatchling shell}}{\text{Volume of 4-inch shell}} = \dfrac{1}{64}$;

   $\dfrac{\text{Surface area of hatchling shell}}{\text{Surface area of 4-inch shell}} = \dfrac{1}{16}$

Test B

1. $648\pi \approx 2035.8 \text{ ft}^3$ **2.** $192\pi \approx 603.2 \text{ in.}^3$

3. $\dfrac{1210\pi}{3} \approx 1267.1 \text{ mm}^3$ **4.** $57.6\pi \approx 181.0 \text{ ft}^3$

5. $\dfrac{62{,}500\pi}{3} \approx 65{,}449.8 \text{ cm}^3$

6. $\dfrac{19{,}652\pi}{3} \approx 20{,}579.5 \text{ mm}^3$

7. $2\sqrt{\dfrac{7433}{14\pi}} \approx 26.0 \text{ in.}$ **8.** $\sqrt{\dfrac{2199}{7\pi}} \approx 10.0 \text{ ft}$

9. $\dfrac{3}{10}$ m   **10.** 15 mm

11. The volume increases by a factor of 12.

12. $90\pi \approx 282.7 \text{ cm}^3$

13. $512 - 32\pi \approx 411.5 \text{ in.}^3$

14. no   **15.** yes

16. $V \approx 936.3 \text{ ft}^3$

17. $S = 358.4 \text{ mm}^2$ **18.** 10 in.

19. There is 1000 times as much sand now. Because the cones of sand are similar,

   $\dfrac{\text{Amount of sand now}}{\text{Amount of sand later}} = \left(\dfrac{10}{1}\right)^3 = 1000.$

20. a. no   **b.** 35.2 times

Alternative Assessment

1. a. *Sample answer:* Cylinder 1 has a larger radius than Cylinder 2. So, Cylinder 1 will have the greater volume.

   b. Cylinder 1: about 471.2 in.^3

   Cylinder 2: about 282.7 in.^3

   Sample answer: Yes, the prediction in part (a) was correct.

Answers

2. a. *Sample answer:* Cone 2 has a larger radius than Cone 1. So, Cone 2 will have the greater volume.

    b. Cone 1: about 134.0 in.^{3}

    Cone 2: about 268.1 in.^{3}

    Sample answer: Yes, the prediction in part (a) was correct.

Chapter 9

9.1–9.2 Quiz

1. a. 2008

    b. 47 male teachers

    c. positive linear relationship

2. The scatter plot shows a positive linear relationship. There is an outlier at (24, 48) and a cluster under $y = 20$.

3. The scatter plot shows no relationship. There is a gap between $x = 10$ and $x = 15$.

4. a.

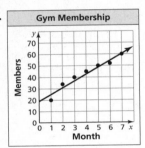

    b. *Sample answer:* $y = 5.9x + 19$

    c. *Sample answer:* The slope is 5.9 and the y-intercept is 19. So, the number of gym members was 19 at the beginning of the time period and increases by about 5.9 per month.

    d. *Sample answer:* about 90 members

9.3–9.4 Quiz

1. a. 34 students   **b.** about 37.8%

    c.

		Sports		
		Involved	**Not Involved**	**Total**
Music Program	**Involved**	62	34	96
	Not Involved	41	27	68
	Total	103	61	164

Sample answer: 164 students were surveyed. 103 students are involved in sports. 96 students are involved in the music program.

2. *Sample answer:* line graph; shows changes over time

3. *Sample answer:* scatter plot; You want to compare two different data sets.

4. *Sample answer:* circle graph; shows data as parts of a whole

5. *Sample answer:* bar graph; shows data in specific categories

6. *Sample answer:* The second interval is larger than the others, making it hard to compare the frequencies.

7. *Sample answer:* The vertical axis has a break and begins at 800,000 dollars. This makes it appear that the account balance decreased rapidly and is almost used up after 5 years.

Test A

1. a. 5 rides

    b. $100

    c. positive linear relationship

2. a.

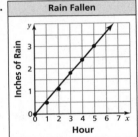

    b. *Sample answer:* $y = 0.6x$

    c. *Sample answer:* The slope is 0.6 and the y-intercept is 0. So, no rain has fallen after 0 hours, and rain falls at a rate of about 0.6 inches per hour.

    d. *Sample answer:* 4.8 inches

3. The scatter plot shows no relationship. There is a cluster under $y = 40$.

4. The scatter plot shows a positive linear relationship. There is an outlier at (27, 45) and a gap between $x = 33$ and $x = 42$.

5. *Sample answer:* line graph; shows how data changes over time

6. *Sample answer:* histogram; shows the frequency of different intervals of ages

Answers

7. *Sample answer:* circle graph; shows the amount of each kind of revenue as part of a whole

8. *Sample answer:* The largest group has too many subcategories compared to the other groups.

9. *Sample answer:* Each icon represents the same number of items. Because the piano icon is larger than the saxophone icon, it looks like the number of pianos is about the same as the number of saxophones.

10. **a.** 12 students   **b.** 52 students   **c.** 60 students

    d.

		Breakfast		
		Ate	Skipped	Total
Lunch	Ate	40	12	52
	Skipped	8	0	8
	Total	48	12	60

    Sample answer: 48 students ate breakfast. 52 students ate lunch.

    e. 20%

Test B

1. **a.** 2013

   b. 325 hybrid vehicles

   c. positive linear relationship

2. **a.**

   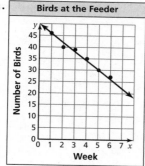

   b. *Sample answer:* $y = 50 - 4x$

   c. *Sample answer:* The slope is -4 and the y-intercept is 50. So, there were 50 birds one week before week 1 and the number of birds decreased by about 4 per week.

   d. *Sample answer:* about 58 birds

3. The scatter plot shows a negative linear relationship. There is an outlier at (24, 20) and a gap between $x = 10$ and $x = 20$.

4. The scatter plot shows a nonlinear relationship. There is a cluster under $y = 40$.

5. *Sample answer:* bar graph; shows data in specific categories

6. *Sample answer:* box-and-whisker plot; shows the variability of a data set using quartiles

7. The first and largest group, 1–6, has many more outcomes than the others—1, 2, 3, 4, 5, and 6, while the other groups have only 2 outcomes.

8. The vertical axis has a break and begins at 19,000. This makes it appear that the number of votes cast increases rapidly from year to year.

9. **a.**

		Visited an Amusement Park		
		Yes	No	Total
Student	Boys	38	17	55
	Girls	29	25	54
	Total	67	42	109

   b. *Sample answer:* 109 students were surveyed. 67 students visited an amusement park. 55 boys and 54 girls were surveyed.

   c. boys: 69.1%; girls: 53.7%

Alternative Assessment

1. **a.** The data shows a positive linear relationship.

   b–c.

   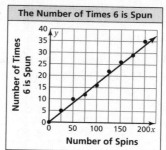

   d. $y = \dfrac{4}{25}x$

   e. *Sample answer:* 48 times

Chapter 10

10.1–10.4 Quiz

1. $\left(\dfrac{1}{5}\right)^5$ 2. $(-2)^3$ 3. y^6 4. $4^3 c^2$

Answers

5. 16 **6.** -27 **7.** $\dfrac{1}{3}$ **8.** 1

9. $(-1)^5$ **10.** b^8 **11.** $64f^3$ **12.** $\dfrac{9}{64}t^4$

13. $(-2)^5$ **14.** 5^7 **15.** x^8 **16.** y^4

17. $\dfrac{4}{c^3}$ **18.** $\dfrac{1}{3x^3}$

19. no; By the Product of Powers Property, you are supposed to add the exponents. x^3x^5 is equivalent to x^8.

20. $x = 5$

10.5–10.7 Quiz

1. no; The factor is less than 1.

2. no; The factor is greater than 10.

3. -0.027 **4.** 4,000,000

5. 3.1×10^{-3} **6.** 7.41×10^5

7. 3.08×10^7, 3.88×10^7, 3.9×10^7

8. 8.1×10^{-5}, 6.5×10^{-4}, 5.2×10^{-3}

9. 4.47×10^3 **10.** 8.61×10^{-3}

11. 4.8×10^2 **12.** 5×10^{-6}

13. 2.0×10^{18} **14.** 3192.6 gal

15. a. 4×10^9 mm

   b. closer; The numbers have the same factor and the exponent 8 is less than the exponent 9.

Test A

1. $\dfrac{1}{27}$ **2.** 32 **3.** 81

4. 6 **5.** 17 **6.** $\dfrac{13}{16}$

7. a. 2.2 million viewers

   b. $2(1.1)^4$; 2.9 million viewers

8. a. no; Replace t with $2t$ and simplify: $d = 5(2t)^2 = 20t^2$. This is four times as much as the original distance.

   b. 60 m

9. $81x^4$ **10.** 2 **11.** $\dfrac{64}{a^2}$

12. $9x$ **13.** $32x^5y^3$ **14.** w^{10}

15. 2000 times larger **16.** 10^{-9}

17. $\dfrac{8}{w^5}$ **18.** $\dfrac{10}{x^{10}}$

19. $\dfrac{1}{8f^2g^5}$ **20.** 50,000

21. 0.00079 **22.** 69,990,000,000

23. 1.33×10^{-2} **24.** 3.77×10^6

25. 1.54×10^{15} **26.** 2×10^{-8}

27. a. 3.6×10^4 to 9.0×10^4 (°F) **b.** cooler

28. 1.4×10^5 km **29.** 1000 times

30. a. 1×10^2 yd by 1.5×10^2 yd by 3×10^1 yd

   b. 4.5×10^5 yd^3

   c. 50,000 yd^3

Test B

1. 49 **2.** -243 **3.** $\dfrac{124}{125}$

4. $\dfrac{31}{36}$ **5.** 448 **6.** $-\dfrac{1}{64}$

7. a. $\dfrac{3}{4}$ mi **b.** $\dfrac{1}{2}(1.5)^5$; 3.8 mi

8. a. no; Replace v with $3v$ and simplify: $E = 25(3v)^2 = 9 \bullet 25v^2$. This is nine times the original kinetic energy.

   b. 630 joules

9. $\dfrac{9w^2}{16}$ **10.** 27 **11.** $\dfrac{b^3}{8}$

12. $\dfrac{125}{a}$ **13.** $-72x^7$ **14.** 1

Answers

15. 200,000 times larger   **16.** 10^{-4} m^2

17. $\dfrac{z^2}{2}$ **18.** $\dfrac{60}{x^{11}}$ **19.** $\dfrac{1}{a^5 b^3}$

20. 7,050,000   **21.** 0.2   **22.** 477,300,000

23. 3.155×10^7 **24.** 5.95×10^{-3}

25. 2.49×10^{-2} **26.** 4×10^2

27. a. 4.6×10^7 km to 6.98×10^7 km   **b.** yes

28. 0.3 mm

29. a. 1×10^{-1} cm by 3×10^{-1} cm by 5×10^{-2} cm

   b. $1.5 \times 10^{-3} \text{ cm}^3$

   c. 50 pieces

Alternative Assessment

1. a. $x^2 y^{-3} = \dfrac{9}{8}, \; x^{-2} y^3 = \dfrac{8}{9}, \; x^2 y^3 = 72,$

$x^{-2} y^{-3} = \dfrac{1}{72}, \; \dfrac{x^2}{y^{-3}} = 72, \; \dfrac{x^{-2}}{y^3} = \dfrac{1}{72},$

$\dfrac{x^2}{y^3} = \dfrac{9}{8}, \; \dfrac{x^{-2}}{y^{-3}} = \dfrac{8}{9}$

b. *Sample answer:* Some expressions are equivalent; some are the reciprocals of each other. The first and second expressions are reciprocals; the third and fourth expressions are reciprocals; the fifth and sixth expressions are reciprocals; the seventh and eighth expressions are reciprocals; the first and seventh expressions are equivalent; the second and eighth expressions are equivalent; the third and fifth expressions are equivalent; and the fourth and sixth expressions are equivalent.

c–d. *Answer should include, but is not limited to:* The two new values will reflect the same relationships as in parts (a) and (b).

e. If the expressions are simplified algebraically so that all exponents are positive, the same relationships will be observed.

$x^2 y^{-3} = \dfrac{x^2}{y^3}, \; x^{-2} y^3 = \dfrac{x^{-2}}{y^{-3}} = \dfrac{y^3}{x^2},$

$x^2 y^3 = \dfrac{x^2}{y^{-3}}, \; x^{-2} y^{-3} = \dfrac{x^{-2}}{y^3} = \dfrac{1}{x^2 y^3}$

2. a. $4.37 \times 5.9 \times 10^{12} = 25.783 \times 10^{12}$
$= 2.5783 \times 10^{13}$ international miles

b. *Sample answer:* It is faster to use scientific notation than to write out the standard form with all the zeros.

c. 25,783,000,000,000 international miles

d. *Sample answer:* It is sometimes hard to compare numbers with many places, whether they are very large or very small numbers. Being able to compare numbers by looking at a single-digit number to the left of the decimal point and an exponent means that you do not have to align decimal points or count the number of zeros. It is easier to see that 1,600,700,803,000 is greater than 1,607,008,003 when they are expressed as 1.6×10^{12} and 1.6×10^9.

End-of-Course Test 1

1. $x = -6$ **2.** $c = 4$ **3.** 300 min

4. a. $A = \dfrac{1}{2} bh$ **b.** $h = \dfrac{2A}{b}$ **c.** 6 in.; 15.24 cm

5. EH **6.** $70°$

7. $A'(-1, -5), \; B'(0, -4), \; C'(-4, -2)$

8. $x = 4, \; y = 4.5$; ratio of perimeters, $2 : 1$; ratio of areas, $4 : 1$

9. yes; ratio, $6 : 1$

10. $62°$ **11.** $135°$

12. 4; Measure 2 in each triangle. The third angle of each triangle can be found by subtracting the sum of the measures of the first two angles from $180°$.

13. slope: 3; y-intercept: -2

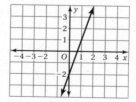

14. slope: $-\dfrac{1}{2}$; y-intercept: $\dfrac{3}{2}$

Answers

15. *x*-intercept: 4; *y*-intercept: 10; 4 adults can attend the play for $20 or 10 children can attend the play for $20.

16. $y = -x + 1$ **17.** $y = -2.5x + 6.5$

18. a. $y = \dfrac{9}{5}x + 32$

   b. $\dfrac{9}{5}$ or 1.8; 1°C corresponds to 1.8°F.

   c. 32; 0°C corresponds to 32°F.

19. $(-1, 1)$ **20.** no solution   **21.** $(-2, -2)$

22. 30 text messages and 25 pictures

23. **Input, *x***   **Output, *y***

24. a.

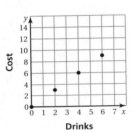

   b. $y = \dfrac{3}{2}x$ **c.** $4.50

25. linear   **26.** nonlinear

27. 4   **28.** 5   **29.** 13 ft

30. 6 and 7; $36 < 42 < 49$, so $\sqrt{36} < \sqrt{42} < \sqrt{49}$.

31. $200\pi \approx 628.3$ in.³   **32.** $75\pi \approx 235.6$ mm³

33. $288\pi \approx 904.8$ cm³

34. a–b.

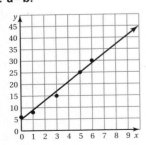

c. *Sample answer*: $y = 4x + 5$

d. *Sample answer*: $21 per hour

35. circle graph; A circle graph shows data as parts of a whole.

36. line graph; A line graph shows how data changes over time.

37. $\dfrac{1}{9}$ **38.** $\dfrac{1}{12}$ **39.** 49

40. 4.6×10^{-10} **41.** 3.5×10^{13}

End-of-Course Test 2

1. $r = -2.4$ **2.** $c = -2.5$ **3.** 145 min

4. a. $A = \dfrac{1}{2}bh; \ h = \dfrac{2A}{b}$ **b.** 6.4 in.; 16.256 cm

5. FG **6.** 60°

7. $A(1, 0)$, $B(0, -1)$, $C(4, -3)$

8. $x = 4.5$, $y = 1$; ratio of perimeters, 3 : 1; ratio of areas, 9 : 1

9. yes; ratio, 3 : 2, or 1.5 : 1

10. 118°   **11.** 144°

12. 4; Measure 2 in each triangle. The third angle of each triangle can be found by subtracting the sum of the measures of the first two angles from 180°.

13. slope: 1.5; *y*-intercept: 1

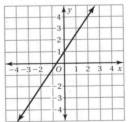

14. slope: $-\dfrac{3}{5}$; *y*-intercept: $\dfrac{1}{5}$

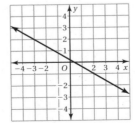

Answers

15. x-intercept: 6; y-intercept: 14; 6 adults can attend the play for $21 or 14 children can attend the play for $21.

16. $y = -3x + 2$ **17.** $y = -2x + 7$

18. $x = 32$ **19.** $\left(-\dfrac{3}{2}, -\dfrac{1}{4}\right)$ **20.** no solution

21. $\left(3, -\dfrac{1}{2}\right)$ **22.** 26 text messages

23.   **Input, x**   **Output, y**

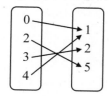

24. a.

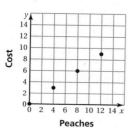

   b. $y = 0.75x$ **c.** $4.50

25. linear   **26.** nonlinear   **27.** -10.2

28. -13 **29.** 25 ft

30. -7 and -6; $-49 < -42 < -36$, so $-\sqrt{49} < -\sqrt{42} < -\sqrt{36}$.

31. $972\pi \approx 3053.6$ in.³   **32.** $120\pi \approx 377.0$ mm³

33. $972\pi \approx 3053.6$ cm³

34. a–b.

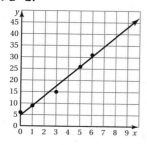

   c. *Sample answer:* $y = 4.25x + 4.75$

   d. *Sample answer:* about $22 per hour

35. circle graph; A circle graph shows data as parts of a whole.

36. line graph; A line graph shows how data changes over time.

37. $-\dfrac{1}{27}$ **38.** $\dfrac{1}{144}$ **39.** 36

40. 1×10^{-4} **41.** 9×10^{-18}